Clodagh's Kitchen Diaries

Clodagh McKenna

Clodagh's Kitchen Diaries

Delicious recipes throughout the year

Clodagh McKenna

First published in Great Britain in 2012 by
Kyle Books
23 Howland Street
London W1T 4AY
general.enquiries@kylebooks.com
www.kylebooks.com

10 9 8 7 6 5 4 3 2 1

ISBN 978-0-85783-147-7

Text © 2012 Clodagh McKenna
Book design © 2012 Kyle Books Limited
Photography © 2012 Kate Whitaker, except page
277 © Ruth Monahan

Project editor: Emma Bastow
Designer: Lucy Parissi
Home economist: Lizzie Harris
Prop stylist: Penny Markham
Editorial assistance: Fiona Rose
Production: Gemma John and Nic Jones

A Cataloguing in Publication record for this
title is available from the British Library.

Colour reproduction by ALTA London
Printed in Spain by Indice Arts Gràfiques
- Barcelona

CONTENTS

INTRODUCTION

As I write this book I think to myself, so why a diary? Well, the last few years it has felt like someone pressed fast forward on my life. I am always on the move. I love change and new experiences, and luckily for me my work is all about that. The only thing is, with the frantic pace I do forget details of these wonderful experiences. Last year was no exception with the opening of my Homemade Food Court, Clodagh's Kitchen Restaurant and my Bakery in Dublin; trips to America to promote my TV series *Clodagh's Irish Food Trails*; the cookery school classes and in-store demonstrations; all alongside the regular day-to-day work. The diary started as an itinerary-come-memory-aid but has ended up being so much more.

I have always associated memorable events and times in my life with food. I remember family birthdays by the cakes my mother baked and holidays by the local food we ate. As food is the filter through which I see and understand the world, it made sense for my diary to take the form of a food journal.

I have been keeping the journal for a couple of years now and it is incredibly useful for looking back and taking stock, and also for planning forward.

Flicking back through last year's pages I get a real sense of the changing seasons and the availability of certain foods in particular months. It's great to look back to January when I need a bit of motivation to keep healthy. A makeover might be a great short term pick-me-up, but feeding yourself well is a fundamental way of increasing your wellbeing in the long term. The January chapter is packed with great tasting superfood recipes to keep you on track throughout the year.

Planning ahead I notice how much of the seasonal celebrations, holidays and occasions with friends and family centre around food. I've included menu plans for Christmas, Easter, New Year and, of course, Valentine's. I love the sense of upholding these traditions with a meal. It binds people together and gives us a sense of continuity.

So back to my original question: why a diary? Reading back over last year I realise it is not just a record of meals eaten or events attended. Each page is filled with memories of the people I celebrated and shared food with and the wonderful places I have lived and eaten in, from Dublin, London, NYC, Italy and France. Here's to another great year and many more meals to come.

Roasted Thyme Turkey

Homemade Cinnamon, Pumpkin and Cranberry Granola

JANUARY

SUPERFOODS

Are you one of those people who, after a couple of thoroughly indulgent nights... weeks... maybe months... resolves to turn your life around? You will eat only whatever the fashionable superfood of the moment is and start achieving optimal performance from your body and mind, starting Monday. Then Monday passes and you promise to do it from the first of the next month. That deadline slips and now you're focussing on the first of January. Sound familiar? Me too.

I read an article about celebrity relationships with food. One very fit celebrity said she didn't "eat for pleasure", that food was simply "fuel for my body". Wow! I would describe my relationship with food as a full blown love affair, one of the great joys in my life. That's when I realised my problem with these superfood diets — I need food to taste great. I think taste is my strongest sense and it just wasn't tempted by the very worthy, but very unappetising, superfood meals available.

Then, at the end of last year I watched a great friend of mine, an avid gym-goer, order the most indulgent meal on the menu. I commented that it made all his work in the gym meaningless. He laughingly replied, "Clo, you've got it the wrong way round. I go to the gym so that I can eat like this". It was a real light bulb moment for me — the ying and yang of eating. If I ate enough of the good stuff — the fibre, the greens, the all-important antioxidants — then I could treat myself to the filet mignon and the glass of Burgundy I occasionally craved.

So, at the end of last year I resolved that from the 1st of January I was going to go for it. I embraced the superfoods but I used them in delicious recipes to keep me motivated. And guess what, very quickly I started to feel a whole lot better. I'm an active, sporty girl and I work hard. Yes, I need my energy tank fuelled but I also need my taste buds tickled. This chapter is filled with recipes using powerfoods without the punishment. Delicious, healthy meals that make you feel great about yourself. Oh and another bonus, I've stuck to my New Year's resolution and it is July when I'm writing this! Easy when eating is about pleasure not denial.

HOMEMADE CINNAMON, PUMPKIN AND CRANBERRY GRANOLA

No shop-bought granola can compare to a homemade version, eated fresh from the oven, still a little warm and melting into your yogurt.

Makes 1kg

100g butter
1 dessertspoon ground cinnamon
150ml clear honey
1 teaspoon vanilla extract
500g rolled oats
150g hazelnuts, roughly chopped
75g pumpkin seeds
75g sunflower seeds
80g desiccated coconut
300g mixed dried fruit (apricots, golden raisins, sultanas, cranberries)

Preheat the oven to 180°C/gas mark 4.

Melt the butter, cinnamon, honey and vanilla extract in a small saucepan.

Put the oats, nuts, seeds and desiccated coconut in a large bowl and pour over the melted butter and honey mixture. Stir well so that all the dry ingredients are evenly coated.

Transfer the mixture to two large baking trays and cook in the oven for 20 minutes, or until golden brown, tossing every 5 minutes. Remove from the oven and leave to cool on the trays, stirring every few minutes.

Remove from the oven and leave to cool on the trays, stirring every few minutes.

Delicious served with low fat yogurt and fresh berries.

BLUEBERRY, CINNAMON AND FLAX PORRIDGE

Buy a big bag of flax for your store cupboard. I use the Linwoods brand — they make a fantastic mixture with goji berries.

Serves 2

200ml water or skimmed milk

80g organic jumbo oats

1 teaspoon ground cinnamon

100g fresh blueberries

1/2 banana, sliced

1 tablespoon ground flax

Put a saucepan over a medium heat and pour in the water or milk (or half of each). Stir in the oats and cook for 5 minutes, stirring occasionally.

Stir in the cinnamon, blueberries, banana and flax, cook for a further minute and serve.

OAT AND CINNAMON HEALTH MUFFINS

Ok, so there is a little brown sugar in this otherwise healthy muffin recipe, but it's a ying-yang muffin!

Makes 8

160g self-raising flour

1 teaspoon bicarbonate of soda

70g porridge oats

140g brown sugar

2 teaspoons ground cinnamon

150ml skimmed milk

6 tablespoons sunflower oil

50g golden raisins

50g walnuts, chopped

Preheat the oven to 180°C/gas mark 4. Line a muffin tin with 8 muffin cases.

Sift the flour and bicarbonate of soda into a large bowl and stir in the oats, sugar and cinnamon. Stir in the milk and oil, then fold the raisins and walnuts into the mixture.

Spoon the mixture into the paper cases, filling them to the brim, and bake in the oven for 20-25 minutes until risen and golden. Serve warm or at room temperature.

CHORIZO AND TOMATO BAKED EGGS

Super simple to make and there are tons of ways
to vary this recipe. Try adding pancetta or sausage,
or whatever you fancy.

Serves 2

25g butter

4 eggs

3 cherry tomatoes,
halved

50g Gruyère cheese (or
another hard cheese,
such as Cheddar or
Gouda), grated

1 teaspoon mustard

2.5cm chorizo,
finely diced

1 tablespoon
double cream

sea salt and freshly
ground black pepper

slices of bread,
toasted, to serve

Preheat the oven to 180°C/gas mark 4.

Grease 2 small ovenproof dishes with the
butter and crack 2 eggs into each one.
Arrange the tomatoes around the eggs.

Put the cheese in a small bowl and mix with
the mustard, chorizo and cream. Season with
salt and pepper. Scoop the cheese mixture
on top of the eggs and bake in the oven
for 10 minutes.

Serve with toasted bread cut into thin slices
so that you can dip them into the eggs.

EGGS FLORENTINE ON TOASTED SESAME BAGELS

Freshly-poached eggs on a toasty bed snuggled up in a blanket of creamy hollandaise. Is there a better way to start the day?

Serves 2

2 eggs
200g baby spinach, steamed and drained on kitchen paper
sesame bagels, cut in half and toasted
100ml hollandaise sauce (see page 91)
sea salt and freshly ground black pepper

There are a couple of tricks to making perfect poached eggs, but for both you should put a large saucepan of cold salted water over a high heat and bring to the boil. When the water is at a rolling boil, stir vigorously with a spoon. While the water is swirling, bring your hands as close as you can to the top of the saucepan and crack your egg into the swirling hot water, which helps bring the egg together. Some people add vinegar, but I prefer the swirling method. Alternatively, you can also crack your egg into a cup and tip it into the boiling water. Allow the eggs to poach for 3 minutes. Once the egg has poached, remove it with a slotted spoon and rest on kitchen paper for 30 second to drain the excess water.

Spoon the steamed spinach on top of the toasted bagels, followed by the poached eggs and then cover with lots of hollandaise sauce. Season with salt and pepper.

OMELETTE FOR ONE

I once stayed in a fishing lodge in Cavan, Ireland, and the wonderful German owner used to make me an omelette every morning. He made it thin and added slices of German salami and Gruyère cheese, to set us up for our day on the lake. I also love cold omelette, sandwiched in sourdough with lashings of homemade mayonnaise.

Serves 1

2 large eggs
60g mature Cheddar cheese, grated
½ spring onion, finely sliced
10ml olive oil
40g mushrooms, sliced (optional)
40g bacon lardons (optional)
¼ red pepper, deseeded and diced (optional)
3 cherry tomatoes, halved
sea salt and freshly ground black pepper
green salad, to serve

Preheat the oven to 180°C/gas mark 4.

Crack the eggs into a mixing bowl and whisk vigorously. Add the cheese and spring onion and season with salt and pepper. Whisk again.

Put a non-stick ovenproof pan over a medium heat and add the oil. Swirl the hot oil around the pan and turn up the heat. If you are adding mushrooms, bacon or red pepper, add them to the pan now and cook for 2 minutes before adding the egg. Tip in the egg mixture, swirling it around the pan to make sure it covers all the pan.

Put the halved cherry tomatoes on one side of the omelette and cook in the oven for 5 minutes. Remove from the oven and use a spatula to flip one side of the omelette on top of the other half and slide on to a plate. I like to eat my omelette with a green salad.

HUMMUS, TZATZIKI AND CORIANDER WRAP

If you are taking this to work for lunch, I would suggest you assemble it just before eating. Salty feta is a delicious addition to this wrap, and if you don't like coriander you can replace with fresh rocket.

Serves 2

2 flour wraps
(use spinach wraps
if you can)
50ml hummus
(see page 166)
50ml tzatziki
(see page 166)
2 sprigs of fresh
coriander, finally
chopped
1/4 cucumber,
finely sliced
100g salad leaves

Open out the wraps. Divide the remaining ingredients equally between them, placing down the middle of the wraps. Roll up the wraps and serve.

BLUEBERRY SUPERFOOD SALAD

Sweet, sweet blueberries. So good for you, and so delicious combined with celery, apple, orange and pomegranite for a super tasty, wholesome salad.

Serves 4

3 tablespoons extra virgin olive oil

1 tablespoon balsamic vinegar

100g fresh blueberries

150g feta cheese, crumbled

1 apple, grated

2 sticks celery, finely sliced

1 orange, peeled and segments quartered, retaining the juice

seeds of 1 pomegranate

50g walnuts, toasted and finely chopped

Whisk together the oil and vinegar.

Put the remaining ingredients in a bowl, mix together and pour the dressing over the salad. Toss well and serve.

POWER ME SALAD

This is the number one selling salad in my restaurants.
Packed with flavour yet light and nutritious, it's the
perfect antidote to the party season.

Serves 2

1 apple, grated
1 carrot, grated
1 beetroot, grated
1/2 fennel, grated
80g salad leaves
80g can chickpeas,
rinsed and drained
juice and zest of
1 orange
juice and zest of 1 lime
50ml extra virgin
olive oil
50g pumpkin seeds,
toasted
sea salt and freshly
ground black pepper

Put the grated apple and vegetables, salad
leaves and chickpeas in a mixing bowl. Add the
juice and zest of the orange and lime along with
the olive oil. Season with salt and pepper and
toss well. Sprinkle the toasted pumpkin seeds on
top and serve.

MOROCCAN SPICED LENTIL SOUP

Serves 6

20ml olive oil
1 onion, finely diced
2 garlic cloves, crushed
10cm piece of fresh ginger, peeled and grated
1.4 litres water
190g red lentils
400g can chickpeas, rinsed and drained
400g can cannellini beans, rinsed and drained
400g can chopped tomatoes
60g carrots, finely diced
60g celery, finely diced
1 teaspoon garam masala
1 teaspoon ground cardamom
$1/2$ teaspoon ground cayenne pepper
$1/2$ teaspoon ground cumin
sea salt and freshly ground black pepper

With a well stocked store cupboard, this will soon become one of your feed-me-and-make-me-feel-good soups.

Put a large saucepan over a medium heat and add the oil. Stir in the onion, garlic and ginger and allow to simmer for 5 minutes.

Add the water, lentils, chickpeas, cannelloni beans, tomatoes, carrots, celery, garam masala, cardamom, cayenne pepper and cumin. Bring to the boil and allow to boil rapidly for a few minutes, then reduce the heat and simmer for 1-1½ hours or longer until the lentils are soft. Taste and season with salt and pepper if needed.

If you want a more rustic soup leave it as is; otherwise, whizz in a food-processor for a smoother consistency.

NUTMEG AND POTATO PANCAKES

Try serving these pancakes alongside meaty, herby sausages and homemade ketchup for a different take on sausage and mash.

Serves 4

450g potatoes, peeled and grated

1 medium onion, grated

2¹/₂ teaspoons freshly ground nutmeg

2 tablespoons plain flour

1 egg, lightly beaten

1¹/₂ tablespoons sunflower oil

sea salt and freshly ground black pepper

Toss together the potatoes, onion, nutmeg, flour and egg in a large bowl. Season to taste with salt and pepper.

Heat ¾ tablespoon of the oil in a large, non-stick griddle or frying pan over a medium-high heat. Drop 3 tablespoons of the potato mixture (1 per pancake) into the pan. Flatten each pancake with a non-stick spatula. Reduce the heat to medium-low and cook for about 5 minutes each side until they are golden brown. Transfer to a plate lined with kitchen paper and keep warm. Repeat, using all the batter and adding additional oil as needed. Serve warm.

ROASTED THYME TURKEY WITH SWEET POTATOES AND ROAST BEETROOT

Many of us tend to only eat turkey at Christmas, but it's an excellent source of lean protein and contains the trace mineral selenium as well as niacin and vitamin B6. Selenium supports the immune system while niacin and Vitamin B6 aid energy production. So there you have it, turkey is a winner all round.

Serves 4

1kg rolled and boned turkey
60ml olive oil
leaves from 2 sprigs of thyme
300g beetroot, scrubbed
1 teaspoon balsamic vinegar
6 sweet potatoes, peeled
1 teaspoon ground cumin
sea salt and freshly ground black pepper

Preheat the oven to 200°C/gas mark 6. Take the turkey out of the fridge and allow it to come to room temperature. Put the turkey into a roasting dish and season with salt and pepper. Mix 20ml of the olive oil with the thyme leaves, spread the oil over the turkey and cook in the oven for 1 hour. (This is 15 minutes for each 450g of turkey and a further 25 minutes.)

Cut the beetroot into large cubes or wedges and put them in a bowl with 20ml of the oil and the balsamic vinegar. Season with salt and pepper, transfer to a roasting tin and cook in the oven for 25 minutes.

Cut the sweet potatoes into wedges and put them in a bowl with the remaining oil and the ground cumin, and season with salt and pepper. Remove the beetroot from the oven after it has been cooking for 5 minutes and mix in the sweet potatoes. Return the tin to the oven and cook the sweet potatoes and beetroot for a further 20 minutes or until cooked.

Allow the cooked turkey to rest for 10 minutes before slicing; if necessary keep it warm by covering it with a tent of kitchen foil. Serve with my delicious Spiced Cranberry Sauce (see page 300).

PAN-ROASTED LEMON AND BASIL SALMON

Also delicious made with haddock, hake or any other fish in season in your part of the world.

Serves 2

2 salmon fillets
8 basil leaves
1 lemon, thinly sliced
50ml olive oil or
rapeseed oil
sea salt and freshly
ground black pepper

Preheat the oven to 180°C/gas mark 4.

Cut the salmon fillets lengthways two-thirds of the way through the centre and open them out. Put 4 basil leaves along the length of each of the opened fillets and put 2-3 slices of lemon on top of the basil. Season with salt and pepper and close the fillets.

Heat a griddle or frying pan over a medium heat, add the oil and swirl it around to coat the pan. Carefully place the salmon, skin side down, in the pan and cook for 3 minutes. Turn the fillets over and put the remaining slices of lemon on top of the salmon. Transfer to the oven and cook for 10 minutes.

The salmon is delicious served with a green salad and Avocado and Beetroot Salsa (see below).

AVOCADO AND BEETROOT SALSA

Serves 4

1 avocado, peeled, stone
removed and diced
1/2 red onion, finely
chopped
200g cooked beetroot,
diced
juice of 1 lime
1 tablespoon balsamic
vinegar
2 tablespoons extra
virgin olive oil
sea salt and freshly
ground black pepper

Put all the ingredients into a bowl and mix well. Season with salt and pepper.

Put the stone of the avocado in with the salsa, cover with clingfilm and store in a fridge. The stone will keep the avocado from turning grey in colour.

BRIOCHE

The smell of fresh brioche wafting from the kitchen is the most incredible aroma. Enjoy with lashings of lemon cured, rhubarb jam or crispy bacon and maple syrup.

Makes 2 loaves

80ml warm water
10g fast-action dried yeast
400g plain flour, plus extra for flouring
1 teaspoon salt
20g white granulated sugar
4 eggs, lightly beaten
220g butter, softened

For the glaze

1 egg yolk
1 teaspoon cold water

Preheat the oven to 200°C/gas mark 6.

Put the water and the yeast in a bowl and whisk together. Leave for 10 minutes until frothy.

Sift the flour into a large mixing bowl and add the salt and sugar. Make a well in the centre and mix in the eggs and the yeast mixture. Beat well until the dough has come together, then turn it out on to a lightly floured surface and knead for about 8 minutes until smooth and supple.

Flatten the dough and spread it with one-third of the butter. Knead this well. Repeat this twice to incorporate the remaining butter, allowing the dough to rest for a few minutes between the additions of butter. This process may take 20 minutes or so. Lightly oil a large bowl, place the dough into the bowl and turn to coat with oil. Cover with clingfilm and leave in a warm place for about 1 hour until it has doubled in volume.

Knock back the dough, cover with clingfilm and refrigerate for 6 hours or overnight. It needs time
to chill in order to become more workable.

Lightly grease two 900g loaf tins. Turn the dough out on to a lightly floured surface and divide it into two equal pieces. Form the pieces into loaves and place them in the prepared tins. Cover with greased clingfilm and leave to rise for about 1 hour until doubled in volume.

Beat the egg yolk with 1 teaspoon of water to make a glaze and brush over the loaves using a pastry brush. Bake for 25 minutes or until the loaves are deep golden brown. Allow the loaves cool in their tins for 10 minutes before removing to wire racks to cool completely.

HEALTH LOAF

This is my Aunt Muriel's recipe. It has now become our house bread in my restaurants and hopefully will in your home, too!

Makes 2 loaves

450g wholemeal flour

65g wheatgerm, plus extra for dusting

65g plain white flour

65g wheat bran

225g pin-head oatmeal

2 teaspoons soft brown sugar

2 teaspoons bread soda or bicarbonate of soda

1 litre buttermilk (see tip on page XX?)

For the topping

2 teaspoons wheatgerm, plus extra for dusting

2 teaspoons sesame seeds

Preheat the oven to 230°C/gas mark 8.

Put all the dry ingredients in a large bowl and mix together. Stir in the buttermilk to make a moist dough.

Lightly grease two 900g loaf tins and dust them with wheatgerm. Divide the dough between the tins, smooth the top and make a cross on each one with a floured knife. Sprinkle with wheatgerm and sesame seeds.

Cook the loaves in the oven for 10 minutes, then reduce the temperature to 130°C/gas mark 1 and bake for 1 hour.

When the loaves are cooked, remove from the oven and leave in the tins to cool a little. Turn them out on to partly cool in the tins, then turn them out on to wire racks to cool completely.

GREEN DETOX JUICE

I do my best to get to my friend Oliver McCabe's Select Stores in Dalkey, Dublin, once a week for his Green Detox Juice. I always feel wonderful afterwards. This juice is fantastic for detoxifying and cleansing the system, and if you are on a serious health plan I would suggest you have this every morning to start your day.

Serves 1

3 apples
½ cucumber
handful of spinach
small bunch of parsley
dash of wheatgrass and spirulina

Juice the apples, cucumber, spinach and parsley and blend with the wheatgrass or spirulina. Pour into a chilled glass and enjoy.

SUPERFOOD SNACK MIX

Last year I started to leave little bowls of raw,
unsalted and unsweetened nut and dried fruit mixes
around the house and office, so that when I was peckish I
could reach for an energy-boosting snack rather than
chocolate bars that just give me a high and then slow me
down. You can mix whatever nuts and dried fruits listed
below (keep clear of raisins as they contain a lot of
natural sugars) and if you are having a chocolate
craving add a square of good quality dark chocolate with
cocoa solids above 70 per cent.

walnuts
whole almonds
hazelnuts
pumpkin seeds
sunflower seeds
goji berries
dried unsweetened
cranberries
dried unsweetened
blueberries
acai berries

Use whatever quantities or combinations of the nuts
and fruit you like. Simply stir gently to combine and
divide into bowls or airtight containers then keep a
stash in your handbag or desk drawer for an instant
energy boost.

BLOOD ORANGE MIMOSAS

The flavour of blood oranges in place of regular oranges in this mimosa is really something special, and the colour is so inviting. A great pick-me-up to combat the January blues.

Serves 8

500ml freshly
squeezed blood
orange juice
1 bottle of chilled
dry prosecco
red blood orange
segments, to garnish
(optional)

Fill 8 Champagne flutes one-third full with blood orange juice and top up with prosecco.

Garnish with a segment of blood orange, if liked, and serve. A great way to cheer-up a dreary January weekend.

Red Velvet Cupcakes

Skinny Fries

FEBRUARY

VALENTINE'S DAY

One Valentine's weekend, I was instructed to pack my case and have my passport ready. It was only when we reached the boarding gate that I knew we were en route to Paris. Two hours later I was tucked away in Le Bar of The George V hotel, sipping on a brandy and Champagne cocktail, pinching myself to make sure I wasn't dreaming. The great cities of the world all have their own spirit; New York buzzes with ideas, London is both regal and irreverent, but there is only one word for Paris: romantic. I was living the dream.

The next morning we walked from the lavish George V to the red banquettes and mahogany tables of Café de Flore on the Left Bank. We sat where Satré and Camus used to sit and ordered the famous *Jambon et Fromage* omelette. We spent hours alternating between coffee and pastis, just watching the world go by. From a famous coffee house to the famous salon de thé Ladurée on Champs-Élysées, well-known for making the first and best macaroons in the world. They were like Paris itself; elegant, exquisite and hopelessly romantic.

We can't all catch a plane to Paris but we can all recreate the romantic atmosphere. Pop a truffle in your lover's pocket when they leave for work. In the afternoon send him or her a menu card for dinner via pic on your phone. Light candles, put scent in your hair and play something French. Have everything prepared beforehand so that you can give them your undivided attention and a delicious cocktail when they arrive. And sweet nothings sound so much more romantic whispered in French - *Que mes baisers soient les mots d'amour que je ne te dis pas.*

Serves 4

20g butter

1kg carrots, chopped

200g onions, chopped

2 garlic cloves, crushed

10cm piece of fresh ginger,
peeled and finely chopped

700ml hot vegetable stock

300ml cream

sprig of fresh coriander,
finely chopped (optional)

sea salt and freshly ground
black pepper

CARROT AND GINGER SOUP

Carrot also tastes great with orange — to make carrot and orange soup, omit the ginger and replace 200ml of the stock with fresh orange juice.

TIP

Store all your butter wrappers in a container in the fridge. When you are sweating vegetables, tuck the butter wrapper around them and they will sweat beautifully.

Melt the butter in a heavy-bottomed saucepan over a medium heat. Add the carrot, onions, garlic and ginger, season with salt and pepper and stir well. Cover, reduce the heat to low and leave to cook for about 15 minutes, stirring occasionally.

Stir in the hot vegetable stock and bring the soup to the boil. When the carrot is tender the soup is ready to be blended. Stir in the cream and coriander and remove from the heat. Blend the soup in a food processor or with a hand-held stick blender until smooth.

SPINACH, TOMATO AND RICOTTA PASTA BAKE

This spinach, tomato and ricotta sauce is really versatile – try using it to stuff cannelloni, or simply combine with pasta for a quicker version of this dish.

Serves 6

600g penne pasta
50ml olive oil
1 onion, thinly sliced
2 garlic cloves,
    finely sliced
2 x 400g cans chopped
    plum tomatoes
pinch of sugar
leaves from 2 sprigs
    of basil
30g butter
300g spinach,
    thoroughly washed
¼ nutmeg, grated
400g crumbly ricotta
80g grated Parmesan
    cheese
sea salt and freshly
ground black pepper

Preheat the oven to 180°C/gas mark 4.

Fill the largest saucepan you have with cold water and add a pinch of salt. Cover and bring to the boil. When the water is at a rolling boil, stir in the pasta and leave to cook for 3-4 minutes. (It should be just al dente as it will cook further in the oven later.) Drain and rinse under cold running water.

Make the tomato sauce by placing a saucepan over a low heat. Add the oil, followed by the onion and garlic. Leave to cook for a minute, then stir in the tomatoes, sugar and basil. Season with salt and pepper.

Meanwhile, put the butter in a frying pan and add a handful of spinach and the nutmeg. Cook the spinach, turning it over as it cooks, and add more as it wilts until all of the spinach is in the pan.

When the spinach is cooked, chop it up finely and mix with the tomato sauce and ricotta. Stir in the pasta, mix well and scoop into a large baking dish. Sprinkle the Parmesan over the pasta and cook in the oven for 15 minutes.

LEMONGRASS AND GINGER INFUSED CRÈME BRÛLÉE

If you're a fan of crème brulee, I suggest investing in a little blow torch. I love mine – I even use it as a weapon to scare grazers out of my kitchen!

Serves 6

10cm piece of fresh ginger, peeled and chopped

2 lemongrass stalks, chopped

100ml milk

1 vanilla pod, split

300ml double cream

6 eggs

100g caster sugar (or vanilla sugar if you have it), plus extra for sprinkling

Preheat the oven to 150°C/gas mark 2.

Put the ginger and lemongrass in a food-processor and whizz to a paste (alternatively grind to a paste using a pestle and mortar).

Put a saucepan over a low heat and pour in the milk, vanilla pod and cream. Stir in the ginger and lemongrass paste and heat gently until hot but not boiling.

Crack the eggs into a large mixing bowl, add the sugar and whisk until fluffy. Slowly pour the hot cream over the egg mixture, mixing vigorously. Strain the mixture through a fine sieve into a medium shallow ovenproof dish and bake for about 40 minutes or until set.

Remove from the oven and allow to cool. Sprinkle with sugar and caramelise using a blowtorch.

CRÊPES SUZETTE

A classic desset: sweet, delicate and lip-smacking. If you can, make the batter the night before as it will be much easier to work with.

Serves 4

juice and zest of
2 oranges
175g caster sugar
75g butter
80ml Cointreau
butter or oil,
for greasing

For the batter

130g plain flour
2 eggs
280ml milk
1 tablespoon melted
butter

First make the crêpe batter. Put the flour into a large bowl and make a well in the centre. Break the eggs into the centre and gradually mix in the flour. Pour in the milk a little at a time, whisking continuously. Put in the fridge to settle for 1-2 hours. Just before you want to use the batter, stir in the melted butterto help prevent the batter from sticking to the pan.

Put the orange juice and zest in a small saucepan with the sugar and butter. Put over a high heat until the butter has melted, then reduce the heat and allow to simmer for 10-15 minutes. At this stage the sauce should be quite syrupy.

Preheat the oven to 150°C/gas mark 2. Put a frying pan (or a crêpe pan, if you have one) over a medium heat and grease with a little butter or oil. Pour a ladle of batter into the pan, and allow to cook for 1-2 minutes, then flip it over and cook on the other side. The crêpe should be a golden brown. Repeat with the remaining batter to make 8 crêpes.

Fold the crêpes into quarters and transfer to an ovenproof dish. Pour the orange syrup over the crêpes and put in the oven for 3 minutes. Meanwhile pour the Cointreau into the small saucepan and heat. Once the crêpes are warmed, pour the liqueur over the crêpes and carefully flambé by lighting with a match. As soon as the flames have died down, transfer to serving plates.

CHOCOLATE, ORANGE AND CARDAMOM PANCAKES

To make flavoured sugar, add a few cardamom pods, vanilla pods, lavender sprigs or star anise to a jar of caster sugar and leave to infuse for a couple of days.

Serves 4

For the batter

130g plain flour, sifted
2 eggs
180ml milk
zest and juice of 1 orange
2 tablespoons melted butter, plus extra for frying

For the sauce

225g good-quality dark chocolate, broken into pieces
60g flavoured sugar, or caster sugar
10 cardamom pods, crushed and seeds taken out (you use the seeds)
50ml cream
zest and juice of ½ orange

Make the pancake batter as for Crêpes Suzette (see page 45), adding the orange juice and zest with the milk, and leave in the fridge to settle.

Meanwhile, make the sauce. Put all the ingredients for the sauce into a saucepan over a gentle heat and stir until the chocolate has melted. Set aside.

When the batter has rested for 1 hour, take it out of the fridge and give it a good whisk. Heat a 20cm (8in) non-stick frying pan and add just enough melted butter to glaze the pan. Swirl the pan to coat evenly with butter.

Preheat the oven to 150°C/gas mark 2. Pour enough batter to cover the pan and swirl around to get an even spread. Cook for 1-2 minutes, flip over the pancake with a spatula and cook for 1 minute on the other side. Transfer to a warm plate, cover with kitchen foil and put in the oven to keep warm. Continue until you have used all of the batter.

Reheat the sauce over a low heat; if it has thickened whisk in 1-2 tablespoons water. Pour the sauce over the pancakes and serve.

ITALIAN SALAD WITH PARMA HAM, PINE NUTS, PARMESAN AND GOAT'S CHEESE CROSTINIS

This salad will only take you about five minutes to prepare. It's light and tasty, perfect as a Valentine's Day starter or a quick lunch.

Serves 2

1 small focaccia loaf, sliced
80g goat's cheese
100g rocket salad leaves
50g pine nuts
50g Parmesan cheese shavings
10 sun-blushed tomatoes
6 slices of prosciutto

For the dressing

50ml balsamic vinegar
150ml extra virgin olive oil
$\frac{1}{2}$ teaspoon Dijon mustard
$\frac{1}{2}$ garlic clove, crushed

First make the salad dressing. Put all of the ingredients into a bowl and mix well. (If you wish to store the dressing, transfer to a sterilised jar and it will keep in the fridge for 1 month.)

Preheat the oven to 180°C/gas mark 4. Smear the goat's cheese onto the focaccia slices and roast in the hot oven for about 5 minutes until toasted.

Meanwhile, put the rocket leaves, pine nuts, Parmesan shavings and sun-blushed tomatoes into 2 large serving dishes and add the salad dressing. Add 3 slices of prosciutto to each salad and serve with the goats' cheese crostinis.

FILET MIGNON

Serves 2

2 filets mignons, each
about 175g
1 tablespoon olive oil
50g butter
1 sprig rosemary, leaves
removed and chopped
1 garlic clove, crushed
sea salt and freshly
ground pepper

Preheat the oven to 200°C/gas mark 6.

Take the steaks out of the fridge 30 minutes before
you're going to cook them. This will allow the meat to
relax so you get a more tender result. Season with
salt and lots of pepper.

Put an ovenproof frying or griddle pan over a medium
heat and add the olive oil and butter. When the butter
has melted add the rosemary and garlic. Turn up the
heat a little and sear the steaks on both sides (about
2 minutes per side) so that they are nicely browned.
Transfer to the oven and cook for 4-5 minutes for
medium rare.

Serve with my Skinny Fries (see page 53), green beans,
chargrilled asparagus or buttered nutmeg spinach and
Béarnaise Sauce (see below).

BÉARNAISE SAUCE

Serves 2

4 tablespoons white wine
vinegar
1 shallot, finely chopped
175g butter
3 egg yolks
1 tablespoon finely
chopped tarragon
sea salt and freshly
ground black pepper

Put the vinegar, shallot and 4 tablespoons of water in
a saucepan over a medium heat to simmer for 3 minutes
or until reduced by one-third. Remove from the heat.

Melt the butter in a separate pan.

Put the egg yolks into a food-processor and whizz.
Slowly pour the melted butter into the egg yolks,
continuing to process, until the mixture is creamy and
thick. Stir in the shallots and tarragon and season
with salt and pepper.

Serve warm. If the sauce separates add a cube of ice
and whisk vigorously.

THE PERFECT SKINNY FRIES

No, unfortunately they won't make you skinny, but they are so good, especially when dipped in béarnaise sauce, that you won't care. You can, of course, deep-fry these chips, but I don't own a deep fryer so I make them in a shallow pan. Although the recipe suggests using fresh rosemary, you could use 1 tablespoon of the dried herb instead. Whenever I'm in New York I buy a tin of dried rosemary from Dean and Deluca, which sells wonderful dried herbs and spices. So go on, dip and enjoy and forget about those skinny jeans for just one evening.

Makes enough for 2 greedy skinny fry lovers

rapeseed or sunflower oil, for frying
4 large baking potatoes, cut into long skinny chips (leave the skin on as it adds flavour and is a good source of fibre)
1 tablespoon olive oil
2 sprigs of rosemary, leaves removed and finely chopped
sea salt and freshly ground black pepper

Preheat the oven to 200°C/gas mark 6.

Put a frying pan on the hob and fill two-thirds full with oil. Turn the heat up as far as it will go.

Dab the raw potato with kitchen paper to remove any excess moisture. When the oil is hot, use a slotted spoon to place a batch of fries into the oil. They should take 4-5 minutes to cook. Work in as many batches as you need to cook all the fries.

Remove from the oil and toss in olive oil, rosemary and salt and pepper. Cook in the oven for 5 minutes.

RED VELVET CUPCAKES

A clever little tip is to crumble one of your un-iced cupcakes into fine crumbs and sprinkle on top of the icing to make a pretty decoration.

Makes 24 cupcakes

30g cocoa powder

3 tablespoons red food colouring

1½ teaspoons vanilla extract

110g butter, softened

170g caster sugar

4 egg yolks

240ml buttermilk

250g plain flour, sifted

1 teaspoon baking powder

For the icing

175g butter

175g icing sugar

1 teaspoon vanilla extract

Preheat the oven to 180°C/gas mark 4. Line two 12-hole cupcake tins with paper cases and set aside.

Put the cocoa, food colouring and vanilla extract in a small bowl and mix well. Put the butter and sugar in a large bowl and use a hand-held mixer to beat them together. Add the yolks and beat for 1 more minute. Add in the cocoa mixture and continue to mix for another minute. Slowly mix in the buttermilk, followed by the flour and baking powder.

Fill each paper case with 3 tablespoons of the mixture and bake for about 15 minutes or until a toothpick inserted in the centre comes out clean. Allow to cool a little in the tins then transfer to a wire rack for 15 minutes before icing.

Make the icing by beating together the butter, icing sugar and vanilla extract to give a thick, creamy consistency. Either put the icing in a piping bag or dip a spoon in hot water and smear the icing on the cupcakes. Decorate with cake crumbs.

Makes 24 macaroons

For the shells

110g ground almond

160g icing sugar

100g egg white (about 3 extra large eggs)

60g caster sugar

½ teaspoon rosewater essence

liquid red food colouring

For the filling

80ml double cream

100g white chocolate, cut into small pieces

20g butter, diced

1 tablespoon rosewater essence

ROSEWATER MACAROONS

Macaroons can be a bit tricky to make, but if you are a keen baker you should definitely try them. Just ensure you make them a cool area, as the shells can melt.

Preheat the oven to 130°C/gas mark 1. Line two medium baking trays with baking parchment or prepare non-stick baking mats.

First make the macaroon shells. Sift the ground almond and icing sugar together into a large bowl and set aside. Beat the egg white using an electric mixer on a high speed until foamy, then gradually add the caster sugar and rosewater essence. Continue beating the egg white until it forms glossy stiff peaks. Add the liquid colouring a drop at a time, stirring well after each addition, until the desired colour is achieved.

Mix the egg white into the ground almond mixture and continue to mix the egg white with the dry ingredients until well combined. The mixture should be thick, glossy and well-blended and look like a thick cake batter.

Next is the fun part! Spoon the mixture into a piping bag fitted with a plain 1cm nozzle. Pipe the mixture on to the lined baking trays or mats,

making macaroons about 2.5cm across and spacing them about 2.5cm apart. Tap the trays on the work surface a couple of times to flatten the macaroons and remove any air bubbles. Leave the shells, uncovered, at room temperature for about 1 hour or until you can touch the shells without them sticking to your fingers.

Meanwhile, make the filling. Put the double cream into a saucepan over a low heat. When it comes to the boil, remove from heat and stir in the white chocolate pieces. Stir the mixture until the chocolate is completely melted. Stir in the butter and rosewater essence and mix until well combined. Chill the filling for at least 1 hour until firm.

Cook the macaroons for about 15 minutes. Transfer the macaroons to wire racks cool (you may need to use a knife to lift the macaroons). When they are completely cool, sandwich two shells together with the chocolate filling. Store in an airtight container in the fridge.

RHUBARB AND GINGER JAM

A handy tip is to use the top of a teaspoon to peel
fresh ginger. It's easier to get around the knobbly
bits and it's so much faster than a peeler.

Cut the rhubarb into 5cm pieces and put into a
large bowl with the sugar, fresh ginger,
crystallised ginger and lemon zest and juice.
Mix well, cover and set aside for 3 hours or
overnight so that the flavours from the ginger
and lemon infuse into the rhubarb.

Tip the rhubarb and all the juices into a
large, heavy-bottomed saucepan and put over a
medium heat. Stir until the sugar has
completely dissolved and bring to the boil.
Continue to cook for about 15 minutes until
the rhubarb is really tender and has reached
setting point (see Tip, right).

Remove the pan from the heat and leave to one
side for 2-3 minutes before pouring into
sterilised jars. The jam will keep in the
fridge for 1 month.

Makes 4 x 450g jars

1kg trimmed rhubarb
1kg preserving sugar
10cm piece of fresh ginger,
peeled and grated
70g crystallised ginger,
finely chopped
zest and juice 1 lemon

TIP

To test if the jam has
reached setting point,
drop a spoonful onto a
cold saucer. Leave for
30 seconds, then gently
push it with the tip of
your finger. If the jam
wrinkles, setting point
has been reached. If not,
continue to cook for a
further 1—2 minutes and
test again.

RHUBARB AND HAZELNUT CRUMBLE

Individual crumbles served in china cups are perfect for a dinner party. They look so decadent on a saucer with a spoonfull of double cream.

Serves 6

800g rhubarb
80g caster sugar
50ml water
50g crystallised ginger, chopped
double cream, to serve

For the crumble

110g butter, chilled and cut into cubes
180g plain flour
80g hazelnuts, roughly chopped
110g brown sugar

Preheat the oven to 180°C/gas mark 4.

Cut the rhubarb into 10cm pieces and toss in a bowl with the caster sugar. Tip into a roasting tin with the water and cook in the oven for 10 minutes. Fill an ovenproof dish about 4cm deep with the rhubarb.

To make the crumble, rub the butter into the flour, hazelnuts and sugar. Sprinkle the mixture over the rhubarb and bake in the oven for 35-45 minutes. Spoon into 6 china cups and serve with double cream.

RHUBARB AND VANILLA UPSIDE DOWN CAKE

This also works well made with apples in place of the rhubarb. Simply peel, core and slice your apples into thickish slices and make as below.

Serves 8-10

190g butter, softened
110g light brown sugar
450g rhubarb
3 eggs, separated
120g caster sugar
180 plain flour, sifted
2 teaspoons baking powder
120ml milk
1 teaspoon vanilla extract
lightly whipped cream, to serve

Preheat the oven to 180°C/gas mark 4.

Melt 80g of the butter in a 30cm non-stick ovenproof pan and swirl it around to coat the whole pan. Stir in the light brown sugar and cook, stirring, for 2 minutes until the sugar begins to melt. Remove from the heat.

Cut the rhubarb into 10cm pieces and place on top of the sugar mixture in the pan.

Whisk the eggs whites until stiff and gradually beat in half the caster sugar.

Put the remaining butter and caster sugar into a food-processor and beat until light and fluffy. Beat in the egg yolks one at a time. Start to add the flour and baking powder a little at a time, followed by the milk and vanilla extract, mixing until well blended and using a spatula to scrape the mixture from the sides of the bowl so that it is completely mixed in.

Fold in the egg whites. I like to mix in the first spoonful of egg whites and combine before folding in the remainder. Spoon the batter on top of the rhubarb in the pan and smooth it out evenly with the back of a spoon. Bake in the oven for 40 minutes. Test the cake by inserting a skewer into the centre of the cake; if it comes out clean the cake is cooked.

Leave the cake to cool in the pan for 10 minutes, then flip it on to a plate and lift off the pan. Serve with lightly whipped cream.

Mint and Chocolate
Cupcakes

Mini Guinness

MARCH

ST PATRICK'S DAY

When I was a kid I loved St Patrick's Day. The day would start with a breakfast of crispy bacon, potato cakes and soda bread, then off to mass. After church, Mum got the stew started and we made brooches for the parade: Irish flags or a harp. The biggest and best float (hands up if you remember) was the bubble gum float. Pretty girls would throw bucket-loads of bubble gum at the screaming, scrambling kids.

By the time the parade was over I'd be freezing, more often than not soaked to the bone, but as happy as a clam because my pockets were full of bubble gum. Back home the smell of Beef and Guinness Stew would hit us as soon as the front door opened. My mum made the best stew in Ireland, everyone's mum did. She'd cut the carrots into big chunks and let the whole thing cook for at least a couple of hours. She'd serve it with creamy champ, with a blob of butter on top and colcannon.

I'm going to make a confession here: as a kid I never liked Cabbage and Bacon soup, our traditional St Patrick's Day starter. Like all good things it took a while to grow on me. Now, I love it. I've included it it in this chapter, a mixture of Mum's recipe and my own.

CABBAGE AND BACON SOUP

When the NBC Today Show came to Ireland I was very chuffed to be asked to cook something traditionally Irish with a twist for the show. We filmed in a lovely pub in Galway and this is what I cooked for Matt Lauer and Hoda Kotb.

Serves 6

50g butter

100g smoked streaky bacon or pancetta, diced

120g potatoes, peeled and diced

2 garlic cloves, crushed

100g onions, chopped

300ml hot chicken or vegetable stock

2 teaspoons dried oregano

300g tomatoes, chopped

300g cabbage, shredded

sea salt and freshly ground black pepper

Put a heavy-bottomed saucepan over a medium heat. Add the butter, and when it has melted stir in the bacon, potatoes, garlic and onions. Cover and cook for 10 minutes.

Add the stock, oregano and tomatoes and bring to the boil. Tip in the cabbage, reduce the heat and cook for about 5 minutes until all the vegetables are tender. Season to taste with salt and pepper and serve with chunks of buttered bread.

CHEDDAR CHEESE SOUP SCONES

I love matching up little scones with soups, try using different flavours to match the soup that you are serving.

Makes 8 Scones

225g plain flour
1 teaspoon baking powder
pinch of sea salt
50g butter
125g mature Cheddar cheese, grated
1 teaspoon chopped thyme leaves
125-150ml milk
oil, for greasing

Preheat the oven to 200°C/gas mark 6.

Sift the flour, baking powder and sea salt into a bowl. Rub the butter into the flour mixture until it resembles fine breadcrumbs. Stir in two-thirds of the grated cheese, followed by the thyme. Gradually pour in enough of the milk to make a soft dough.

Roll out the dough on a lightly floured surface to about 1cm thick and use a pastry cutter or upturned glass to cut circles. Transfer the scones to a greased baking tray and sprinkle over the remaining cheese. Bake in the oven for 12-15 minutes, then transfer to a wire cooling rack for 5 minutes.

IRISH CHEESE SOUFFLÉS

The secret to making lovely, lofty soufflés is to not be tempted to open the oven before they are ready and to serve them straight from the oven.

Makes 4 soufflés

30g butter, plus extra for greasing
2 tablespoons plain flour
250ml milk, warmed
120g Coolea cheese, finely grated (this is an Irish cheese — if you cannot find it, use a cheese like Gouda instead)
½ teaspoon ground nutmeg
4 large eggs, separated
sea salt and freshly ground black pepper

Preheat the oven to 200°C/gas mark 6. Butter 4 individual ramekins.

Put the butter in a saucepan over a low heat. When it has melted, stir in the flour and continue to stir until a roux forms. Whisk in the milk a little at a time until you have a creamy sauce.

Stir in the cheese and nutmeg and mix well. Beat in the egg yolks, one at a time, then remove the saucepan from the heat and continue to stir for a few minutes. Season with salt and pepper.

Whisk the egg whites to stiff peaks, then fold them into the cheese mixture. Fill the ramekins with the soufflé mix and immediately bake in the oven for 25 minutes. Be careful not to open the oven door for the first 20 minutes, or the soufflés will flop.

POTATO CAKES

You can make this the night before and then just reheat in the oven the next day. Sometimes I add grated Cheddar cheese or finely chopped pancetta to the potato mix.

Makes 6 potato cakes

1kg potatoes, peeled
100ml crème fraîche
1 egg yolk
1 teaspoon Dijon mustard
2 tablespoons chopped spring onions, steamed shredded cabbage or steamed leeks
2 tablespoons plain flour
30g butter
sea salt and freshly ground black pepper

Cook the potatoes in a large saucepan of boiling salted water until tender. Drain, transfer to a bowl and mash with a potato masher.

While the potatoes are still hot mix in the crème fraîche, egg yolk, mustard and salt and pepper. Mix in the spring onions, cabbage or leeks.

Add 1 tablespoon of the flour to the mixture to help make the consistency suitable for rolling out and sprinkle the remaining flour on your work surface. Roll the potato mixture out to 5cm thick using a rolling pin and cut it into circles using a 10cm scone or biscuit cutter.

Melt the butter in a frying pan and fry the potato cakes on both sides until golden brown.

HONEY-GLAZED BACON
STUFFED WITH APPLE

If you can't get your hands on a loin of bacon, then used a piece of smoked or un-smoked gammon.

Serves 8

1.4 kg loin of bacon (if the rind is on, make sure you ask your butcher to score it)

salt and pepper

For the glaze

50g butter

300g cooking apples, peeled, cored and chopped

1 onion, finely chopped

5cm piece of fresh ginger, peeled and grated

80g brown sugar

$\frac{1}{2}$ teaspoon chilli powder

4 cloves

100ml cider vinegar

sea salt and freshly ground black pepper

Preheat the oven to 190°C/gas mark 5.

First make the glaze. Put the butter in a saucepan over a medium heat. When the butter has melted stir in the apples, onion and ginger, season with salt and pepper and cook for 3 minutes. Add the sugar, chilli powder and cloves, stir well, cover and cook for 3 minutes.

Pour in the vinegar, bring to the boil and simmer for about 20 minutes. Use the back of a wooden spoon to mash up the apples so the mixture is nice and thick. At this stage you can transfer the mixture to a sterilised jar and it will keep for up to 3 months.

Remove the loin of bacon from of the fridge and cover it with the spiced apple. Cook in the oven for 1 hour 40 minutes, basting every 20 minutes.

GUINNESS AND BEEF STEW

The longer and the lower temperature that you cook this stew, the better the flavour. I recommend that you make it the day before you plan to eat it as the flavours concentrate much more.

Serves 8

25g butter
150g bacon lardons
300g shallots, left whole
1kg stewing beef, cubed
400g mixed wild mushrooms
1 litre Guinness
1 bouquet garni
sea salt and freshly ground black pepper

Preheat the oven to 160°C/gas mark 3.

Put the butter in a frying pan over a medium heat. When the butter has melted add the bacon, followed by the shallots. Cook until golden brown and transfer to a large casserole.

Add the beef to the frying pan, season with salt and pepper and cook until browned all over. Transfer to the casserole.

Add the mushrooms to the pan and cook for 2 minutes. Season to taste and transfer to the casserole.

Return the frying pan to the heat and use a whisk to scrape off all the bits stuck to the bottom of the pan (this is where the flavour is). Pour in the Guinness and continue to whisk for another minute to deglaze the pan. Pour the Guinness and pan juices over the beef and vegetables in the casserole. Add the bouquet garni, cover the casserole and cook in the oven for 2 hours.

Check the seasoning, remove the bouquet garni and serve with roast potatoes.

MINT AND CHOCOLATE CUPCAKES

These are just so cute! I box them up and give them to my friends on St Patrick's Day. We can't make enough of these in my bakery on Paddy's Day.

Makes 18 cupcakes

225g self-raising flour
1 teaspoon baking powder
4 tablespoons cocoa powder
225g unsalted butter
225g caster sugar
4 eggs
1 teaspoon mint essence
100g plain chocolate chips

For the decoration

225g icing sugar, sifted
1 teaspoon mint essence
115g unsalted butter, softened
green food colouring
100g plain chocolate chips

Preheat the oven to 180°C/gas mark 4. Line an 18-hole cupcake tin with paper cases.

Sift the flour, baking powder and cocoa into a bowl.

Put the butter and sugar into another bowl and use an electric whisk to beat them together until light and fluffy. Add the eggs one at a time, beating the mixture as you go, then stir in the mint essence and chocolate chips. Fold in the flour mixture and mix well.

Spoon the cake mixture into the cases and bake in the oven for about 20 minutes or until a toothpick inserted into the centre comes out clean.

Meanwhile, make the icing. Whisk together the icing sugar, mint essence and butter. Stir in just enough food colouring to turn the icing mint green. Ice the cooled cakes and decorate the tops with chocolate chips.

IRISH COFFEE

Ok, I'm an Irish gal and a chef, so if I can't make a
good Irish Coffee, well... This traditional Irish tipple
is too good to be served just once a year on St
Patrick's Day – they are a lovely way to finish a dinner
party and are a great pick-me-up on a cold and gloomy
winter evening.

Makes 1

30ml Irish whiskey
2 teaspoons brown sugar
100ml good-quality
strong coffee
cream

Carefully warm a glass. Add the Irish whiskey to the
warmed glass and stir in the sugar.

Pour in the coffee and, using the back of a spoon,
pour the cream onto the surface of the coffee.

TIPS

Mini Guinness can be made ahead and stored in the fridge for 24 hours.

You could use espresso cups, china tea cups or martini glasses.

There are lots of variations you can try: omit the espresso coffee and fold in raspberries, or 1 teaspoon cardamom seeds, or the juice and zest of 1 orange.

MINI GUINNESS

This mousse is light and fluffy yet rich thanks to the good quality chocolate. I suggest that you use chocolate that has 70 per cent cocoa solids.

Makes 12 shot glasses

200g good-quality chocolate
100ml double cream
1 teaspoon caster sugar
4 eggs, separated
100ml good-quality strong espresso coffee, cold

To serve

200ml whipped double cream
grated chocolate or chocolate-coated coffee beans

Break the chocolate into a heatproof bowl suspended over a saucepan of simmering water. Melt the chocolate, stirring often to make sure that no lumps form.

Remove the bowl from the heat and stir in the cream, sugar, egg yolks and coffee.

In a clean bowl whisk the eggs whites until stiff peaks form. Fold the egg whites into the chocolate mixture. Pour the chocolate mixture into individual shot glasses and put in the fridge for 1 hour or until they are set.

Before serving top with whipped double cream and decorate with a grating of chocolate or chocolate-coated coffee beans.

MOTHER'S DAY

On Mother's Day I like to make my mum a beautiful afternoon tea. After all it was from her I learned my love of baking. When I was little she would bake every Saturday morning for the week ahead, filling the house with a delicious buttery, vanilla smell. I'd watch from my stool, desperate to have a go on the hand-held whisk or to turn the dial on the Kenwood mixer.

One year I did a Mother's Day tea for friends who were young mums. I invested in a mini cupcake stand and spent a heavenly morning decorating the cakes with icing sugar flowers and butterfly decorations. You can buy amazing cupcake decorations in most good food stores. I used my prettiest china and linen and decorated the table with small jam jars of wild flowers. You can buy beautiful little doilies that are perfect for large cakes or tarts and look gorgeous. It was a real treat but also felt a bit naughty and decadent.

At Clodagh's Bakery in Arnott's we do a Mothering Sunday high tea. Our famous Buttermilk Scones are very popular, so too is my mum's favourite Lemon Drizzle cake. Just in case you fancy impressing mum with your home baking, I've included recipes from The Bakery in this Chapter. The main thing is not where you take your mum or the cakes, it's spending time with your mum and making her feel precious and appreciated.

EGG MAYO MINI ROLLS

An afternoon classic. The key is not to overcook the eggs.
I find 6 minutes in boiling water cooks them perfectly.

Makes 6

3 eggs at room
temperature
½ tablespoon butter
1 tablespoon mayonnaise
3 chives, finely sliced
6 mini rolls
sea salt and freshly
ground black pepper

Put a saucepan of cold water over a medium heat and
bring to the boil. When the water is boiling carefully
add the eggs and simmer for 6 minutes. Drain the eggs
and cool under cold running water. Remove the shells.

Mash the eggs together with the butter, mayonnaise,
chives and season with salt and pepper.

Cut the mini rolls in half, spoon the egg mayonnaise
onto the bottom halves and replace the top halves.

ROAST BEEF AND HORSERADISH
MINI ROLLS

Perfect for leftover roast beef. When I cook roast beef
at home half way through dinner I'm already planning
this sandwich for the following day.

Makes 12

200ml crème fraîche
3 tablespoons
horseradish, grated
½ teaspoon Dijon
mustard
juice of ½ lemon
12 mini rolls
24 rocket leaves
6 thin slices of roast
beef, halved
sea salt and freshly
ground black pepper

Put the crème fraîche, horseradish, mustard and lemon
juice in a bowl, season with salt and pepper and mix
well.

Cut the mini rolls in half. Put 2 rocket leaves on the
bottom halves. Top with a piece of beef and add dollop
of the horseradish cream. Replace the top halves of
the rolls.

CUCUMBER, SALMON AND CREAM CHEESE SANDWICHES

Use good organic or wild smoked salmon for this. I'm lucky to live in Ireland where we have some of the worlds best fish smokers.

Makes 32 small rectangular sandwiches

8 slices of wholegrain bread

100g cream cheese, softened

200g smoked salmon

½ cucumber, thinly sliced

sea salt and freshly ground black pepper

Smear the bread with cream cheese.

Layer a slice of smoked salmon and a few slices of cucumber on 4 slices of the bread and season with salt and pepper. Sandwich together with the remaining slices of bread.

Use a serrated knife to cut off the crusts. Cut each sandwich diagonally into quarters.

MINI JAM TARTS

You may not use all the jam but it's better to have 2 jars just in case as you don't want any tarts going unfilled! You can freeze the un-cooked pastry cases.

For the pastry

220g plain flour, plus extra for dusting

110g unsalted butter, chilled and diced, plus extra for greasing

1 teaspoon golden caster sugar

1 egg yolk

2 tablespoons cold water

For the filling

2 jars of good quality strawberry or raspberry jam

Preheat the oven to 180°C/gas mark 4. Lightly grease and dust two 12-hole mini tart trays.

To make the pastry, sift the flour into a large bowl and rub in the butter with your fingertips (if you prefer, you can whizz the butter and flour together in a food-processor). The mixture should resemble fine breadcrumbs. Mix in the sugar.

Mix in the yolk, add the water and knead the mixture until it forms a dough. Wrap it in clingfilm and put in the fridge to chill for 30 minutes.

Roll out the dough on a lightly floured surface to about 4mm thick and cut out 24 small circles with a biscuit cutter. Put the pastry circles over each hole of the tart trays and gently push the pastry into the hole. Use a fork to prick a few holes in each tart case. Bake in the oven for 5 minutes, remove and fill with the jam. Return to the oven for a further 10 minutes.

Allow the tarts to cool in the tins for 5 minutes, then remove to a wire rack to cool completely before serving.

Makes 24 scones

900g self-raising flour,
plus extra for dusting

1 teaspoon baking powder

80g caster sugar

500ml buttermilk or full-fat
milk, plus extra for glazing

300g butter, softened

30g sultanas

OUR FAMED BUTTERMILK SCONES

Have light hands with the dough and don't over work it
or you won't get a light fluffy scone. You can substitute
the sultanas for raisins, cranberries or blueberries.

Preheat the oven to 240°C/gas mark 9. Lightly dust two baking
trays.

Sift the flour and the baking powder into a large mixing bowl
and mix in the sugar. Make a well in the centre and slowly
pour in the buttermilk or milk, using your other hand to mix
the milk into the flour as you pour. Stir in the sultanas.

Using floured hands, bring the dough together and roll it out
to about 2.5cm thick. Use a scone cutter to cut out the scones
and put onto the baking trays.

Brush with a little milk and bake in the oven for 5 minutes.
Reduce the temperature to 160°C/gas mark 3 and cook for a
further 20 minutes.

COFFEE, WALNUT AND CARDAMOM CAKE

I love coffee cake in the afternoon with freshly brewed tea — add cardamom to the mix and I'm in afternoon heaven. If you are not as big a fan of cardamom as I am, just omit it.

Serves 8-10

200g butter at room temperature
200g caster sugar
3 eggs
200g self-raising flour
1 teaspoon baking powder
seeds from 10 cardamom pods, crushed
40ml espresso coffee
80g walnuts, finely chopped

For the icing

300g icing sugar
200g butter
100ml espresso coffee
1 teaspoon cardamom seeds, crushed
6 walnuts, halved

Preheat the oven to 180°C/gas mark 4. Grease and line the base and sides of a 20-22cm round cake tin.

Put the butter in a large mixing bowl with the sugar and beat together with a whisk until light and fluffy.

Slowly beat in the eggs, one at a time. When the eggs are fully incorporated, fold in the flour, baking powder, cardamom seeds, coffee and walnuts.

Pour the cake mixture into the tin and tap the sides to release any air bubbles. Bake in the oven for 35-40 minutes or until the sponge is lightly golden brown. Check by inserting a skewer into the middle of the cake; if it comes out clean the cake is cooked.

Meanwhile, make the icing. Whisk together the icing sugar, butter, coffee and cardamom seeds until you get a light and fluffy icing.

Leave the cooked cake to cool for 10 minutes in the tin, then remove to cool completely on a wire rack. Cut horizontally through the centre of the cake.

Spread half of the icing on the top of the bottom half of the cake. Place the top half in position and cover with the remaining icing. Decorate the top with the halved walnuts.

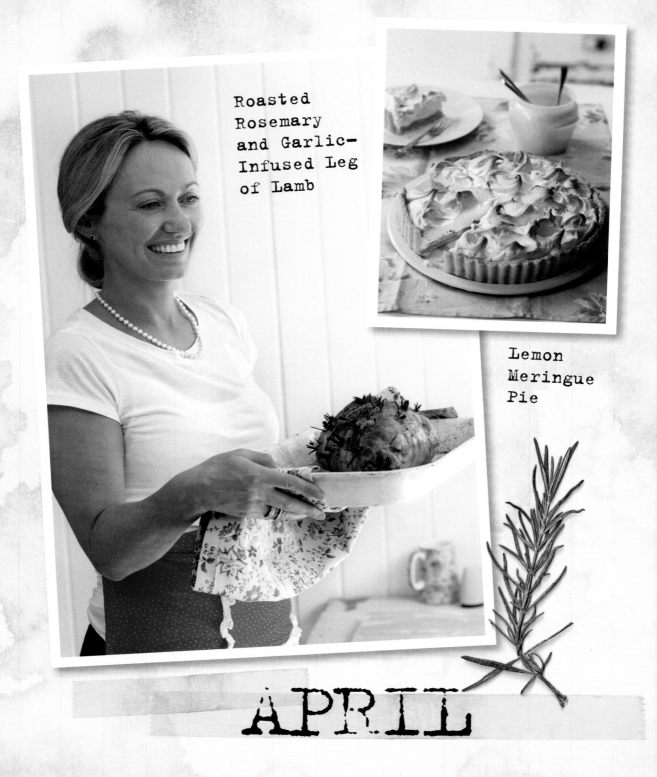

Roasted
Rosemary
and Garlic-
Infused Leg
of Lamb

Lemon
Meringue
Pie

APRIL

NEW YORK

I got a call to appear and give a cookery demonstration on the
Rachael Ray show in the USA. They also wanted to show a clip
of my series *Clodagh's Irish food Trails* which was airing on
the PBS network over there. I was thrilled. Rachel Ray is
massively popular — a celebrity chef, author and television
personality — and it was a great opportunity to promote the
show. No worries.

It was only when I got out of the car on Madison Avenue that I
realised just how big Rachael Ray is. Her name is emblazoned
across the front of the building where the show is shot. People
were queuing round the block to be in the studio audience. I
thought my heart was going to leap out of my chest.

Rachael completely put me at ease, making me feel like I was
in her kitchen, just sharing tips with a fellow cook. I cooked
my Roast Rosemary and Garlic-Infused Leg of lamb, followed by
Coffee Chocolate Mousses, with a white chocolate froth on top.
You guessed it, like a glass of Guinness! I was keen for the
presentation to reflect my vintage style. Her fantastic
stylists found beautiful fifties martini glasses to serve the
mousse in. I was really pleased with the result. The glasses
gave the dessert a real elegance. I still can't believe it all
happened. I have to watch the recording to remind myself it
really did.

ASPARAGUS, MINT AND RICOTTA TARTLETS

Super simple to make and so tasty. Use asparagus in the recipe while it's in season, but you can substitute with lots of other vegetables when it isn't, such as tomatoes or courgettes.

Makes 4

1 sheet of ready-rolled all-butter puff pastry
150g ricotta
80g Parmesan cheese, finely grated
finely grated rind of 1 lemon
8 asparagus spears
olive oil, for brushing
sea salt and freshly ground black pepper
mint leaves, to serve

Preheat the oven to 200°C/gas mark 6. Line a baking tray with non-stick baking parchment.

Cut out four rectangles, each 12 × 6cm, from the pastry sheet and place them on the baking tray. Score a 1cm border on each rectangle.

Put the ricotta, Parmesan, lemon rind, salt and pepper into a bowl and stir to combine. Spoon the mixture on to the pastry and top each tart with two asparagus spears. Brush the pastry borders with oil and cook in the oven for 12-15 minutes or until the pastry is puffed and golden.

Serve with a couple of mint leaves on top.

GOOD FRIDAY FISH – ROASTED HAKE WITH MINTED HOLLANDAISE SAUCE

I eat a lot of fish, being the granddaughter and niece of fishermen and also making two TV series and writing a cookbook on the subject. You are going to love my foolproof recipe for hollandaise sauce – I promise you it won't split! You can substitute the mint for basil, tarragon or any herb you like.

Preheat the oven to 180°C/gas mark 4.

Season the hake on both sides with salt and pepper. Put an ovenproof pan over a medium heat and pour in the olive oil. When the oil is hot add the fish, skin side down, and sear for 2 minutes. Turn over and sear the other side for 2 minutes before placing in the oven for 10 minutes.

Meanwhile, make the hollandaise sauce. Heat the butter in a saucepan over a low heat until melted. Pour the egg yolks and lemon juice into a food-processor. Set the food-processor to a medium speed and slowly pour in the melted butter until all the butter is well blended with the egg yolks and the sauce is thickened.

Toss the asparagus in a little olive oil, season with salt and pepper and roast in the oven for 8-10 minutes. Serve with minted new potatoes.

Serves 2

2 fillets of hake
50ml olive oil, plus extra for tossing
10 asparagus spears
sea salt and freshly ground black pepper

For the hollandaise sauce

200g butter
5 egg yolks
juice of 1 lemon
leaves from sprig of mint, finely chopped

91

ROASTED ROSEMARY AND GARLIC-INFUSED LEG OF LAMB

I made this wonderful Easter Sunday lunch when I was a guest on the Rachel Ray Show in the US. It was so exciting to have been asked on the show, the energy from everyone working behind the scenes was incredible!

Serves 6

2kg leg of spring lamb
small bunch of rosemary
3 garlic cloves, sliced
olive oil
sea salt and freshly
ground black pepper

Take the lamb out of the fridge 30 minutes before you intend to cook it. This will allow the meat to relax, so that it will be more tender when it is cooked.

Preheat the oven to 200°C/gas mark 6.

Put the lamb in a roasting tin and score the fat, then make several deep incisions across the top with a sharp knife. Push small pieces of rosemary, each about 5cm long, and a slice of garlic into each incision. Rub a small amount of olive oil over the skin and season with salt and pepper.

Roast the lamb for 20 minutes, then reduce the temperature to 180°C/gas mark 4 and cook for a further 1 hour for rare, 1¼ hours for medium and 1½ hours for well done.

When the lamb is cooked remove it from the tin, cover it with a tent of kitchen foil and allow to rest for 15 minutes before carving.

THE ULTIMATE GRAVY

This is a gravy recipe I use for most of my roasts. I vary the wine and cream depending on how rich or light I want the gravy to be to match the piece of meat. Make it your own by adding different herbs or wines.

Serves 6

100ml red wine (optional)
600ml chicken stock
2 garlic cloves, left whole
leaves from 1 sprig of rosemary, finely chopped
50g butter
50g flour
100ml cream (optional)
sea salt and freshly ground black pepper

When you have taken the meat out of the roasting tin, pop the tin over a medium heat. If you are using red wine (I highly recommend it) add it to the pan and use a whisk mix it with the juices. Leave to simmer for 3 minutes to allow the alcohol to evaporate.

Add the stock, cloves and rosemary and bring to the boil. Whisk in the butter and flour to thicken the gravy slightly. Pour in the cream (optional, but adds a lovely richness).

Taste and allow to bubble up until the flavour is concentrated enough. Season with salt and pepper and pour through a sieve into your gravy boat.

ZIPPY FRESH MINT SAUCE

5 tablespoons finely chopped fresh mint
3 tablespoons white wine vinegar
2 teaspoons caster sugar
1 tablespoon hot water

Put all of the ingredeints into a bowl and whisk well. You have mint sauce — simple!

Serves 10

600g spinach
olive oil, for frying
300g arborio rice
1 onion, finely chopped
8 tablespoons freshly grated
Parmesan cheese
3 eggs, lightly beaten
butter, for greasing
sea salt and freshly ground
black pepper
100g breadcrumbs

ITALIAN EASTER SPINACH AND RICE BAKE

When I lived in Turin in Northern Italy, we used to eat this traditional savoury cake at Easter time. It's a great way to use-up leftover risotto rice. Serve with a big green salad to add a little lightness.

Preheat the oven to 180°C/gas mark 4.

Prepare the spinach by removing and disgarding the stems and rinsing the leaves in cold water. Drain well. Heat a drop of olive oil in a frying pan over a medium heat and cook the spinach until soft. Remove from the pan and chop finely.

Cook the rice according to the packet instructions until al dente, then drain well. Meanwhile place the pan used for the spinach back on the heat and add a drop of olive oil followed by the onion and cook until soft. In a large bowl mix together the spinach, onion, rice, 5 tablespoons of the Parmesan and the eggs, and season wth salt and pepper.

Grease a medium round cake tin with butter and press the rice and spinach mixture into the pan. Sprinkle the breadcrumbs on top followed by the remaining Parmesan. Cook in the oven for 35—40 minutes or until golden.

Serves 6

For the pastry

175g plain flour
100g cold butter, diced
1 tablespoon icing sugar
1 egg yolk

For the filling

1 tablespoon cornflour
juice and zest of 2 large lemons
90g golden caster sugar
80g butter, diced
3 egg yolks and 1 whole egg

For the meringue

4 egg whites
180g golden caster sugar
1 teaspoon cornflour

LEMON MERINGUE PIE

I'm not sure I've ever met anyone who doesn't like Lemon Meringue Pie. To save time, buy a jar of lemon curd instead of making the filling, or just mash up some meringues and fold-in lemon curd with whipped cream.

Preheat the oven to 180°C/gas mark 4.

First make the pastry. Put the flour, butter, icing sugar, egg yolk and 1 tablespoon cold water into a food-processor and mix until combined. Tip the dough on to a lightly floured surface, gather it together until smooth, then roll out and line a 23 × 2.5cm loose-bottomed fluted flan tin. Trim the edges and press the pastry into the flutes. Prick the base with a fork, line with kitchen foil and chill for 1 hour.

Pour baking beans on top of the foil and bake the pastry blind for 15 minutes. Remove and allow to cool.

To prepare the filling, mix together the cornflour, lemon zest and juice and sugar in a medium-sized saucepan. Continue to cook over a medium heat, stirring constantly, until thickened. Remove from the heat and whisk in the butter. Beat together the egg yolks (save the whites for the meringue) and the whole egg, stir into the pan and return to a medium heat. Keep stirring vigorously for a few minutes until the mixture thickens again. Remove from the heat and set aside.

To make the meringue, put the egg whites in a large bowl and whisk to soft peaks, then add half the sugar, a spoonful at a time, whisking after each addition. Whisk in the cornflour, then add the rest of the sugar and whisk until smooth and thick.

Reheat the filling and pour it into the pastry case. Immediately put spoonfuls of meringue around the edge of the filling (if you start in the middle the meringue may sink), then spread it so it just touches the pastry. Pile the rest of the meringue into the centre, spreading so it touches the surface of the hot filling (and starts to cook), then swirl using a knife to form soft peaks. Return to the oven for 18-20 minutes until the meringue is crisp and slightly coloured.

Allow the pie to sit in the tin for 30 minutes, then remove and leave to cool for at least another 30-60 minutes before slicing.

Makes 12

oil, for greasing

240ml milk

1 pack (7g) fast-action yeast

120g caster sugar

300g plain flour

260g strong flour

100g black raisins

2 tablespoons candied lemon peel, cut into 5mm pieces

2 tablespoons candied orange peel, cut into 5mm pieces

$\frac{1}{2}$ teaspoon cinnamon

$\frac{1}{4}$ teaspoon ground nutmeg

pinch of salt

4 tablespoons butter, melted

2 large eggs plus 1 yolk

100g icing sugar

$\frac{1}{2}$ teaspoon vanilla extract

HOT CROSS BUNS

I always used to think hot cross buns were difficult to make, and avoided baking them for years. When I finally gave them a try one Easter, I realised they are really easy to make. They will keep for about 4 days in an airtight container but if they do go a little hard, toast them and spread with lashings of butter.

Preheat the oven to 240°C/gas mark 9. Coat a large bowl with oil and set aside. Line a large baking tray with baking parchment.

To make the dough, whisk together half the milk, the yeast and 1 teaspoon of the sugar in a small bowl and leave to stand until frothy. Combine the flours, remaining sugar, raisins, candied peels, spices and salt in the bowl of a standing mixer fitted with a dough hook and mix on low speed until combined (alternatively add the ingredients to a large bowl and combine by hand). Add the butter, 2 eggs and the yeast mixture and continue to mix for about 3 minutes or until a sticky dough forms.

Transfer the dough to a lightly floured surface and knead by hand for about 5 minutes until smooth. (If you have combined the dough by hand increase the kneading time to 10 minutes.) Form the dough into a ball, place it in the prepared bowl and turn to coat all sides with oil. Cover with a clean, damp tea-towel and leave to rise in

a warm, draught-free place for about 1 hour or until it doubles in volume.

Knock back the dough, place it on a lightly floured surface and knead for 3 minutes. Divide the dough into 12 equal pieces. Shape each piece into a ball and place about 2.5cm apart, in three rows of four, onto the prepared baking tray. Cover and leave to rise for about 1¼ hours until doubled in volume.

In a small bowl combine the egg yolk with 1 tablespoon water. Use a pastry brush to lightly brush the egg mixture on the top of each bun. Place the buns in the oven, reduce the temperature to 200°C/gas mark 6 and bake for about 20 minutes until golden brown. Transfer to a wire rack.

In a small bowl combine the icing sugar, remaining milk and vanilla extract. Stir until smooth. When the buns have cooled slightly, drizzle a horizontal line across each row of buns followed by a vertical line to form a cross on the crown of each one.

OUR FAMED CARROT CAKE

This is most certainly the prized cake of our bakery. Light, fluffy and kissed with spices, you'll be licking your lips and reaching for another slice!

Makes 1 cake

140ml vegetable oil, plus extra for greasing
3 eggs
220g light brown sugar
350g grated carrots
100g golden raisins
100g walnuts, chopped
200g self-raising flour
pinch of salt
1/2 teaspoon bicarbonate of soda
1 teaspoon ground cinnamon
1 teaspoon freshly grated nutmeg

For the icing

300g cream cheese, chilled
70g butter at room temperature
1 teaspoon vanilla extract
300g icing sugar, sifted
finely grated zest of 1 orange

For decoration

walnuts
orange zest

Preheat the oven to 180°C/gas mark 4. Oil a 13 × 23cm loaf tin and line with greaseproof paper.

First make the cake. Beat the eggs in a large bowl, then add the oil, brown sugar, grated carrot, raisins and chopped walnuts. Sift in the remaining ingredients and bring the mixture together using a large spoon until well combined.

Pour the mixture into the prepared loaf tin, smooth the surface and bake in the oven for 1¼ hours or until a skewer inserted into the middle comes out clean.

Remove from the oven and allow the cake to cool in the tin for about 5 minutes before transferring it to a wire rack to cool completely.

To make the icing, beat together the cream cheese and butter in a bowl until well combined. Add the vanilla extract, icing sugar and orange zest and mix until the icing is smooth and thick. Use a palette knife to spread the icing evenly over the cooled cake, dipping the knife into a bowl of hot water if the icing is hard to spread. Decorate the top of the cake with walnuts and orange zest.

MINI CUPCAKES IN AN EGG BOX

How can any other easter gift compare to these?
Too cute.

Makes 48 mini cupcakes

170g butter, softened
170g caster sugar
2 eggs
1 teaspoon vanilla
extract
150ml milk
250g plain flour, sifted
1 teaspoon baking powder

For the icing

175g butter
175g icing sugar
1 tsp vanilla extract
food colouring
(optional)

To decorate and package (optional)

lemon zest
chopped pistachios
chocolate flakes
seeds from vanilla pods
eggs cartons
ribbon

Preheat the oven to 180°C/gas mark 4. Line two 24-hole mini cupcake tins with paper cases and set aside.

In a bowl beat together the butter and sugar using an electric whisk. Add the eggs one at a time and continue to whisk until completely incorporated. Slowly pour in the milk, followed by the flour and baking powder, and whisk to combine.

Fill each paper case with 1 tablespoon of the mixture and bake for about 10 minutes until a toothpick inserted into a cupcake center comes out clean. Allow to cool in the tins for 15 minutes then transfer to a wire rack to cool completely before icing.

To make the icing beat together the butter, icing sugar and vanilla extract until thick and creamy. If you wish you can separate the icing out into different bowls and mix in different food colourings

To ice the cup cakes, either pipe the icing onto the cakes using a piping bag or dip a spoon in hot water and smear the icing onto the cup cakes. Decorate with your choice of toppings.

Pop the mini cupcakes into the egg cartons, close and tie with a pretty ribbon.

DANNY MEYER

Danny Meyer is a New York City restaurateur, author and the CEO of Union Square Hospitality Group. He's a real New York icon and a huge inspiration to me. Any restaurant that Danny Meyers opens is a favourite of mine, from the fun shake shacks to the Union Square Café, but my favourite has always been Maialino, a fabulous Roman-style trattoria at the Gramercy Park Hotel. When I'm in New York I always try and eat at Maialino, and the last time I went for breakfast I enjoyed fantastic ricotta pancakes with poached eggs and tripe and great coffee.

My favourite time to go to Maialino is in the afternoon for a glass of wine and a few small bites from their bar menu, and I can't leave with out having the Baccala, Cotiche Fritte (pork crackling) and their perfectly aged Pecorino cheese. Thank you to Danny and Executive Chef Nick Anderer for their delicious Bucatini All'Amatriciana recipe on page 103.

BUCATINI ALL'AMATRICIANA

Serves 2

50g guanciale or pancetta, diced
small red onion, diced
1 teaspoon dried red chilli flakes
400g tin whole peeled tomatoes
150g bucatini or other long pasta
2 tablespoons olive oil
50g pecorino cheese, grated, plus extra to serve
salt and coarsely ground black pepper

Bring a large pan of salted water to the boil.

Meanwhile gently sautee the guanciale or pancetta in a deep frying pan over medium heat until crisp and brown. Remove the guanciale or pancetta, leaving the fat behind, and set aside. Add the onions to the pan and sautee for several minutes over medium-low heat until soft.

Add salt (keeping in mind that the guanciale or pancetta will be salty), a generous amount of pepper and the chilli flakes, and gently cook for a further 20 seconds, then add the tomatoes. Simmer for 10 minutes, breaking-up the tomatoes with the back of a spoon as they cook, until the sauce thickens.

Meanwhile drop the bucatini into the boiling water and cook until al dente. Drain, reserving a little of the cooking water, and add the pasta and reserved cooking water to the frying pan along with the guanciale or pancetta. Simmer gently, stirring continuously, for a minute or two or until the sauce begins to cling to the pasta.

Add the olive oil and the cheese, stirring well to combine. Serve with extra pecorino on the side.

LEMON ROASTED CHICKEN WITH OLIVE, BASIL & TOMATO SAUCE AND PAN-FRIED GNOCCHI

I love the restaurant Baltazar in New York — the food and atmosphere are great. This my version of a delicious dish that I had the last time I was there.

Serves 4

4 garlic cloves, crushed

juice and zest of 1 lemon

4 tablespoons olive oil, plus extra for frying

4 supreme chicken fillets, skin on

300g ripe plum tomatoes, halved

1 onion, finely chopped

20 black olives, halved

20 basil leaves

25g butter

100g gnocchi

sea salt and freshly ground black pepper

Preheat the oven to 180°C/gas mark 4.

Put 2 of the crushed garlic cloves into a large bowl with the lemon juice and zest, 2 tablespoons of the olive oil and salt and pepper. Stir well to combine, then add the chicken and turn to coat. Cover the bowl and place in the fridge.

To make the tomato sauce, put the tomatoes, cut side up, into a roasting tin and sprinkle over the onion, remaining garlic, olives, basil and the remaining olive oil. Season to taste and cook in the oven for 15 minutes or until the tomatoes have roasted.

Remove the chicken from the fridge and place, skin side down, in a hot frying pan for 3 minutes. Turn and cook for a further 2 minutes. Transfer to a roasting tin and cook in the oven for 15 minutes.

Transfer the roasted tomatoes to a blender and whizz to a smooth sauce.

Put a frying pan over a medium heat and add the butter and a little olive oil. When the butter has melted, tip in the gnocchi, season and cook, tossing every minute, for 5 minutes or until the gnocchi are golden brown.

Spoon a bed of the tomato sauce onto 4 plates, lay the chicken on top and arrange the gnocchi around the chicken.

Makes 24 large cookies

360g plain flour
1 teaspoon baking powder
1 teaspoon salt
220g unsalted butter at room temperature
200g peanut butter
2 teaspoons vanilla extract
200g light brown sugar
100g caster sugar
2 large eggs

PEANUT BUTTER
CHOCOLATE COOKIES

I never leave New York without a trip to Dean and Deluca on Broadway. You'll catch me gobbling their peanut butter cookies and stacking up on spices to bring home.

Preheat the oven to 180°C/gas mark 4. Line two large baking trays with baking parchment.

Mix together the flour, baking powder and salt in medium-sized bowl. Put the butter, peanut butter and vanilla extract in a seperate bowl and beat using an electric whisk until well blended. Beat in both sugars, scraping down the sides of the bowl with a spatula.

Stir half of the dry ingredients into the peanut butter mixture. Add the eggs, one at a time, stirring well after each addition. Mix in the remaining dry ingredients.

Roll 2 heaped tablespoons of dough into a ball about 7.5cm across. Repeat to make around 24 cookies. Arrange the balls 7.5cm apart on the prepared baking trays and use the back of a fork to flatten them. Bake in the oven for about 15 minutes until golden brown. Leave them to cool on the baking trays for about 5 minutes, then use a spatula to transfer them to wire racks to cool completely.

Rose Sangria

MAY

MY BIRTHDAY

You know when your birthday is coming up and you secretly hope
something has been arranged? Well, a couple of years ago that didn't
happen to me. It was an incredibly busy time and my birthday just
came and went. I had cards and calls from family but there was no
actual celebration to mark the day. Boo hoo. I decided that would
never happen again. If I want to celebrate my birthday I will take
responsibility for it myself.

One year I had a tapas party. I whizz round so much with work I
don't always get a chance to catch up with friends, so tapas is a
perfect solution — delicious, easy to make and an incredibly social
and relaxed way to eat. Because it was my birthday everyone was
happy to get involved, pushing the big table against the back wall,
decorating the room and taking the dishes out afterwards. I put a
big bowl of gazpacho in the centre of the table and, to keep things
simple, I focussed on just six tapas dishes but I made sure there
was plenty of them. One thing I learned
is that you can't have enough hot
chorizo, sliced thickly on cocktail
sticks. People love it.

This year, I had a girly lunch on my
actual birthday. It felt so sophisticated
and frothy. Cocktails with salads to
mitigate the sumptuous key lime pie for
pudding, and as a final little feminine
touch banoffi pie cupcakes as favours for
my fabulous girlfriends. So if you don't
think your friends are organising a
fabulous surprise party for your birthday
this year, why not do it yourself. Make
your birthday cake and eat it too!

Makes 1

lots of ice
25ml vodka
100ml good-quality apple juice
thin slice of apple

APPLETINIS

A couple of years ago my friend Giana Ferguson (famed cheeseamaker of Gubbeen cheese) made me a gin version of this drink, which also tasted delicious. Use good quality apple juice or make a sparkling version by using sparkling apple juice. It's a refreshing, perfect pre-lunch tipple!

Fill a cocktail shaker half full with ice and add the vodka and apple juice. Shake, pour and garnish with a slice of apple.

CHICKEN CAESAR SALAD

Caesar salad is all about the dressing. My dressing is so simple to make and it will last in the fridge for about 10 days. I make versions of this salad with prawns and pancetta at my restaurant Clodagh's Kitchen in Dublin. Just omit the chicken and replace with either pan-fried prawns or crispy pancetta. I'm not a lover of croutons and prefer to serve a couple of grissini (breadsticks) with the salad.

Serves 2

1 tablespoon olive oil
2 chicken fillets
1 garlic clove, crushed
1 teaspoon chopped rosemary
10 very ripe cherry tomatoes, halved
20 cos lettuce leaves
1 heaped teaspoon pumpkin seeds
sea salt and freshly ground black pepper

For the dressing

2 tablespoons mayonnaise
1 tablespoon grated Parmesan cheese
1 garlic clove, crushed
1/4 teaspoon Dijon mustard
juice of 1/2 lemon

Preheat the oven to 200°C/gas mark 6.

Put a frying pan over a medium heat and add the oil. Leave to heat for 30 seconds, then add the chicken, season with salt and pepper and sprinkle over the garlic and rosemary. Cook on each side for about 2 minutes until lightly golden. While the chicken is still cooking in the pan, carefully cut it into small pieces and continue to cook for a further 3 minutes.

Meanwhile, make the Caesar dressing. Put all the ingredients in a blender and whizz for 30 seconds.

When the chicken is cooked, remove it from the pan and keep warm in the oven. Add the cherry tomatoes to the frying pan and cook for 2 minutes.

Put the lettuce leaves in a large salad bowl, add the cooked chicken and tomatoes, pour over the dressing and toss well. Sprinkle the pumpkin seeds on top.

CREAMY BASIL AND GRILLED CHICKEN TAGLIATELLE

This is wonderfully creamy but also sweet and fresh, thanks to the basil and tomatoes. Ideal for a girls' lunch or a speedy mid-week supper.

Serves 2

1 tablespoon olive oil
2 chicken fillets
250g rigatoni or penne pasta
12 cherry tomatoes
100ml basil pesto
150ml crème fraîche
50g Parmesan cheese, grated
sea salt and freshly ground black pepper

Put a frying pan over a medium heat, add the oil and leave to heat for 30 seconds. Add the chicken, season with salt and pepper and cook on each side for 5 minutes or until lightly golden. Slice the seared chicken into small pieces and return to the pan.

Put a large saucepan of cold water over a high heat, season with salt, cover and bring to the boil. When the water is at a rolling boil, stir in the pasta and keep stirring for a minute so that the pasta shapes don't stick together.

Cut the tomatoes in half, add them to the frying pan with the chicken and cook for a further 5 minutes.

Mix together the pesto and crème fraîche and stir into the pan with the chicken and tomatoes. Reduce the heat and simmer for 5 minutes.

Drain the pasta and return it to the saucepan. Add the chicken and sauce, stir well and season to taste with salt and pepper. Serve in two large, warm pasta bowls with the grated Parmesan.

BANOFFI PIE CUP CAKES

Wickedly good, I remember the morning when we perfected this recipe in my bakery and that sublime first bite.

Makes 12

For the cakes
2 eggs

80g butter

125g caster sugar

1 teaspoon ground cinnamon

3 very ripe bananas, mashed

150g self-raising flour, sifted

1 teaspoon baking powder

For the caramel
210g sugar

85g butter

120ml cream

For the icing
75g butter

75g caster sugar

Preheat the oven to 180°C/gas mark 4. Line a 12-hole cupcake tin with paper cases.

To make the caramel, put the sugar, butter and cream in a saucepan over a medium heat, stirring all the time. When the mixture has come to the boil, reduce the heat and stop stirring.

To make the cakes, whisk together the eggs, butter and sugar until light and fluffy. Add the cinnamon and bananas, then fold in the flour, baking powder and three-quarters of the caramel.

Spoon the mixture into paper cases until they are about two-thirds full and bake in the oven for 15 minutes. Transfer to a wire rack to cool.

Meanwhile, make the icing. Whisk together the butter and sugar with the remaining caramel. Pipe the icing onto the cooled cakes.

KEY LIME PIE

This should take you no longer than 15 minutes to prepare. You can accessorise the base with hazelnuts or pine nuts, but the filling is perfect and has no need to be dressed in any way. Make the pie the day before you wish to eat it and it will taste even better. It will keep for five days in the fridge.

Serves 8-10

Preheat the oven to 180°C/gas mark 4. Grease a 22cm springform cake tin.

For the base

12 digestive biscuits
45g caster sugar
135g butter, melted, plus extra for greasing

First make the base. Put the biscuits, caster sugar and melted butter in a food-processor and whizz together for 2 minutes. Transfer the biscuit base to the tin and press down with the back of a spoon.

For the filling

4 egg yolks
400ml condensed milk
juice and zest of 5 limes

To make the filling, whisk the egg yolks in a bowl, then gradually whisk in the condensed milk until smooth. Mix in the lime juice. Pour the filling on to the biscuit base and cook in the oven for 15-20 minutes. Transfer to a wire rack to cool.

Sprinkle the lime zest over the pie and serve chilled.

CHOCOLATE BIRTHDAY CAKE

This is so so simple to make. The cake is lovely and light where as the icing is rich an fudgy. It will last for 4 days in the fridge, but hopefully it won't last one day!

Makes 1 cake

Lightly grease and flour two 20cm round cake tins.

For the cake

300g plain flour, plus extra for flouring
1 teaspoon baking powder
1 teaspoon bicarbonate of soda
70g cocoa powder
250g sugar
170g butter, plus extra for greasing
4 eggs
375ml milk
2 teaspoons vanilla extract

First make the cake. Sieve the flour into the bowl of a mixer then add the remaining ingredients. Mix, first on a low speed then increasing to medium, for 4 minutes until the ingredients are well combined.

Divide the mixture between the 2 tins and tap gently to remove any air bubbles. Cook in the oven for 45 minutes or until a toothpick inserted into the centre comes out clean. Allow the cakes to cool in the tins for 15 minutes before removing to a wire rach and leaving to cool completely.

While the cake is cooling make the icing. Whisk all the ingredients together to form a delicious light fudgy icing.

For the icing

220g cream cheese, softened
50g butter, softened
3 tablespoons milk
450g caster sugar
100g cocoa powder
2 tsps vanilla extract

Ice the bottom half of the cake and sandwich the two cakes together, then completely smother with icing.

ROSE SANGRIA

This drink goes down so well, just remember to share it! Try using sparkling wine for a more fun sangria. It needs to be served very cold so add lots of ice to the mix before serving in chilled glasses. I always pop my glasses in the freezer for 30 minutes before use.

Serves 8

1 bottle chilled rosé wine
250ml Cointreau
2 limes, thinly sliced
2 oranges, thinly sliced
16 raspberries, quartered
1 litre sparkling water
lots of ice

Stir together the wine, Cointreau, limes, oranges, raspberries and sparkling water. Add the ice and serve in iced glasses.

SPANISH SPICY GARLIC PRAWNS

For a more sophisticated dish, serve the prawns on slices of toasted baguette brushed with olive oil, or for more of a kick try chilli oil.

Serves 10

8 tablespoons extra virgin olive oil

8 garlic cloves, chopped

3 chillies (hot or mild, to taste), deseeded and chopped

2 tablespoons smoked paprika (or standard paprika)

1 onion, finely chopped

1kg raw peeled king prawns

Heat the oil over a gentle heat and add the garlic, chillies, paprika and onion. Cook until the onion is soft, without any colour.

Add the prawns to the pan and increase the heat slightly. Cook for 5-10 minutes or until the prawns have turned dark pink.

Serve with crusty bread to mop up the flavoursome juices.

CROQUETTES

These are a real crowd pleaser and taste even better if you prepare them the night before and let them set in the fridge overnight before cooking.

Serves 8

300g mashed potato

1 dessertspoon Dijon mustard

1 teaspoon finely chopped flatleaf parsley

200g cooked ham, cut into small pieces

100g Gruyère cheese, grated

1 egg, beaten

200g fine breadcrumbs

olive oil

sea salt and freshly ground black pepper

Preheat the oven to 200°C/gas mark 6.

Put the mashed potato, mustard, chopped parsley, cooked ham and cheese in a large bowl and mix well.

Use a tablespoon to scoop the mixture into cork-like shapes. Lay them on a tray and use a pastry brush to coat each all over with beaten egg. Scatter the breadcrumbs on a large plate and, one by one, gently roll the croquettes in the crumbs.

Fry the croquettes in a frying pan in hot oil, turning them once, until they are golden; alternatively, bake them in the oven for 15 minutes.

TAPENADE TOASTS

Try adding a sliver of Manchego cheese, a teaspoon of soft goat's cheese, or cured ham on top of the toasts.

Serves 10

400g pitted black olives

75g capers, pressed in kitchen paper to remove excess vinegar

50g anchovy fillets, drained

4 garlic cloves

3 tablespoons extra virgin olive oil, plus extra for brushing

juice of 1 lemon

1 baguette, sliced

Put the olives, capers, anchovies, garlic, oil and lemon juice in a food-processor and blitz to a thickish paste, adding more oil if required.

Toast the bread and brush with olive oil. Smear the tapenade on top of the toast and serve.

GAZPACHO

I love serving gazpacho in chilled shot glasses. You can make this ahead and store in a fridge. If your gazpacho gets too thick just whisk in more chilled water.

Serves 8

1kg ripe tomatoes, skinned and chopped

2 garlic cloves, crushed

1 red pepper

1 onion, chopped

1 slice of good-quality stale white bread

250ml cold water

2 tablespoons olive oil

2 tablespoons white wine vinegar

sea salt and freshly ground black pepper

For the garnish

½ cucumber, diced

2 spring onions (scallions), finely chopped

Put all the ingredients in a blender or food processor and process until completely smooth. Transfer to a bowl, cover and leave to chill in the fridge.

Serve chilled, garnished with cucumber and spring onions.

TRADITIONAL SPANISH TORTILLA

Try adding chorizo, pancetta, tomatoes or prosciutto to this fab recipe. It's delicious served cold with a drizzle of homemade mayonnaise or tomato salsa, too.

Serves 2

2 tablespoons olive oil
1 onion, halved and thinly sliced
280g potatoes, peeled and diced
6 eggs, beaten
sea salt and freshly ground black pepper

Place a large frying pan over a medium heat and add 1 tablespoon of the oil. When the oil is hot add the onion and potatoes, reduce the heat and allow to cook for 15 minutes, stirring the pan every few minutes.

When the onion and potatoes are cooked, tip them into a bowl with the eggs. Season with salt and pepper and mix together.

Place the frying pan over a low heat and add the remaining oil. Pour in the egg mixture and leave to cook for about 15 minutes or until the egg is set.

To flip the tortilla over, put a plate over the pan and turn the pan over so that the tortilla comes out on the plate. Slide the tortilla back into the pan, cooked side up, and return to the heat for a further 5 minutes.

You can eat the tortilla hot or cold. It's delicious with a green salad.

SEAFOOD PAELLA

The first time I tasted Paella was in the La Brecha food market in San Sebastian. It really is the best party food and can be made with many different types of fish.

Serves 10

olive oil, for frying
20cm piece of chorizo, diced
(I love Gubbeen chorizo from
Ireland)
2 onions, diced
4 garlic cloves, crushed
500g paella rice
2 teaspoons paprika
1 litre hot fish stock
pinch of saffron
500g monkfish, chopped
1kg mussels, cleaned and
debearded
10 unshelled raw prawns
6 red piquillo peppers
sea salt and freshly ground
black pepper
2 lemons, cut into wedges,
to serve

Heat a large paella pan over a medium heat. Add a little olive oil and the chorizo. Leave to cook for about 5 minutes until the chorizo begins to crisp, then add the onions and garlic. Cook for a further 10 minutes.

Stir in the rice and season with salt and pepper. Add the paprika, stock and saffron and leave to simmer for about 15 minutes.

Scatter the pieces of monkfish over the rice and push them under the surface with the back of a spoon. Lay the mussels and prawns over the top and simmer for another 5 minutes. Lay the piquillo peppers on top to warm through. Cook for a further 5 minutes or until the mussels have opened and the prawns are pink. Discard any mussels that remain closed. Serve with lemon wedges around the pan.

TIPS
You can add mussels, shrimps, hake — practically any kind of fish — to this dish. If you can't get your hands on piquillo peppers, core, deseed and slice some ordinary red peppers and add them along with the onions.

MOROCCAN ORANGE CAKE

This, I guarantee, will be one of your favourite recipes in this book. Light, moist and so zingy, it will keep for up to a week in an airtight container.

Serves 8

50g slightly stale white breadcrumbs
200g caster sugar
100g ground almonds
1 teaspoon baking powder
200ml sunflower oil
4 eggs
finely grated zest of 1 large unwaxed orange
finely grated zest of 1 unwaxed lemon
whipped cream or Greek yogurt, to serve (optional)

For the citrus syrup

juice of 1 unwaxed orange
juice of 1 unwaxed lemon
75g caster sugar
1 cinnamon stick
2 cloves

Preheat the oven to 180ºC/gas mark 4. Line the base and grease and flour a 20.5 × 5cm round cake tin.

Mix together the breadcrumbs, sugar, almonds and baking powder. Whisk the oil with the eggs, then pour the egg mixture into the dry ingredients and mix well. Add the orange and lemon zests. Pour the mixture into the cake tin and cook in the oven for 45-60 minutes or until the cake is golden brown. Check that the cake is cooked by inserting a skewer into the centre; if it's ready the skewer should come out clean. Allow to cool for 5 minutes before turning out on to a wire rack.

Meanwhile, make the citrus syrup. Put all the ingredients into a saucepan and bring gently to the boil, stirring until the sugar has dissolved completely. Simmer for 3 minutes. Remove the cinnamon stick and cloves from the syrup.

While the cake is still warm, pierce it several times with a skewer, then spoon the hot syrup over the cake, allowing it to run into the holes. Leave to cool. Spoon any excess syrup back over the cake every now and then until it is all soaked up. Serve with whipped cream or a dollop of thick Greek yogurt, if liked.

Potted Shrimp

Sparking Summer Berry Jellies

JUNE

SUMMER PICNICS

June is the start of the big summer sporting events.I love the tennis but my real passion is the races - Punchestown, Leopardstown, Galway and, of course, Royal Ascot. The horses are so beautiful, the actual races are ridiculously exciting, but for me the best thing is the picnic. I love seeing people in the car park, the boot open, serving the most sumptuous feasts off the top of the spare tyre. In this chapter I wanted to look at picnic food that isn't just a few snacks but a proper lunch, worthy of the sport of kings.

The trick is to choose food that travels well. To avoid things getting soggy, keep your chutneys, relishes and pickles away from the bread and dressing away from the salad until you are ready to eat. Same with cucumber and tomato, chop them just before serving to avoid watery salads. Keep dishes with a strong or pungent smell wrapped and sealed and make sure your ice packs are frozen hard to keep everything fresh.

A really elegant way to start the picnic is with potted shrimp. Little brown shrimps boiled in spiced sea water on board the boats, then sealed in butter. Serve with Melba toast and squeeze of fresh lemon. Cold meats, whole cooked salmon and quiches travel well and are delicious with salads. A great cheese course always works but not at the expense of something sweet and yummy, and if you serve the sweet stuff with tea, it has to come from a pot and use loose leaf tea, not bags. Just don't get so into the picnic you forget to have a punt!

Makes about 500g
500g pasta flour
a large pinch of salt
2 medium eggs
semolina flour, for
dusting

FRESH PASTA

The feeling of achievement when you roll a pasta sheet into tagliatelle is fantastic. It takes a few goes to get the hang of it but once you have, there's no stopping how creative you can be. Happy pasta making!

Put the flour, salt and eggs in a food-processor and blend together until a dough forms. Put the dough on a floured board and knead until smooth. Separate the dough into six balls, cover with a tea-towel and allow to rest in a cool place or in the fridge for 30 minutes.

If you have a pasta machine, set it up and push the dough through the roller. With each pass through the rollers reduce the setting, until you reach the final setting. Be careful that your pasta does not break as you should now have a long, thin sheet.

If you don't have a pasta maker you need to roll the dough out very thinly with a rolling pin. (This can be hard as it breaks easily, and if you intend to make a lot of pasta I would recommend buying a pasta maker because they are inexpensive and so useful.) Dust lightly with semolina flour and hang over a clean clothes horse or something similar for 10 minutes.

Store in the fridge and eat within 2 days.

To make **lasagne sheets**, cut the pasta into suitably sized rectangles.

To make **tagliatelle**, cut into 1cm strips.

For **tagliolini**, cut the dough into 5mm strips.

For **pappardelle**, cut the dough into 2cm strips

FLAVOURED FRESH PASTA

For **spinach pasta**, take 150g spinach and blanch in boiling water for 1 minute, drain and squeeze dry. Add to the flour and egg and proceed as on page 134.

For **tomato pasta**, add 2 tablespoons of tomato paste to the flour and egg and proceed as on page 134.

For **herb pasta**, add 4 tablespoons of finely chopped herbs of your choice (such as basil, fresh coriander or oregano) to the flour and egg and proceed as on page 134.

For **black ink pasta**, add 3 tablespoons of squid ink to the flour and egg and blend as on page 134; you may need to add a little more flour if the dough is too moist.

To cook the pasta: The best way to cook your pasta is to get the largest saucepan that you have and fill it with cold water and a good pinch of salt. Cover and bring to the boil. Once the water is at a rolling boil tip the pasta into the water and stir immediately for 2 minutes so that the pasta pieces do not stick together. Cooking times vary depending on the shape and size of the pasta, so the best way to check it is to taste it. The pasta should be slightly al dente because it will continue to cook after it has been drained. Drain the pasta, reserving about 2 tablespoons of the cooking water, and return the drained pasta to the saucepan (off the heat). Stir in the 2 tablespoons of cooking water, followed by your pasta sauce.

THREE CHEESE RAVIOLI

You can play around with the combinations of ricotta and spinach, smoked salmon and soft goat's cheese. The ravioli freezes well, so you can make ahead. I love to serve this with a fresh sun-blushed tomato pesto or my creamy coriander and walnut pesto (see page 211).

Serves 2

65g ricotta
65g Parmesan cheese, grated
65g Fontina cheese, grated
½ teaspoon dried oregano
1 tablespoon finely torn basil
1 batch of homemade fresh pasta (see page 134)
sea salt and freshly ground black pepper

In a medium bowl mix together the ricotta, Fontina, Parmesan, oregano and basil and season with salt and pepper.

Use a 7cm cookie cutter cut out circles from your pasta sheets. Put about 2 teaspoons of filling in the centre of half the pasta circles, leaving a clear edge around the perimeter. Dip a pastry brush in water and lightly brush around the edges of each circle. Put one of the remaining pasta shapes on top and press the edges together to seal around the filling, being careful to press out any excess air.

Bring a large saucepan of salted water to boil. Cook the ravioli for about 5 minutes or until al dente. Serve with Creamy Walnut and Coriander Pesto (see page 211) or Olive, Basil and Tomato Sauce (see pages 104).

CREAMY TOMATO AND SPINACH PASTA

A lovely, light summer dish — perfect for enjoying al fresco with a chilled white wine.

Serves 6

olive oil, for frying
1 onion, thinly sliced
2 cloves garlic, peeled and finely sliced
2 x 400g tins good-quality plum tomatoes, chopped
8 basil leaves
600g penne pasta
2 knobs of butter
8 large handfuls of spinach, washed and drained
¼ of a nutmeg, grated
400g crumbly ricotta cheese
sea salt and freshly ground black pepper
2 handfuls of freshly grated Parmesan cheese to serve

Bring a large saucepan of salted water to the boil.

Meanwhile make the tomato sauce. Heat a glug of olive oil in a saucepan over a low heat and add the onion and garlic. Leave to cook for a minute then stir in the tomatoes and basil and season with salt and pepper. Reduce the heat and allow to simmer for 10 minutes or until thickened.

Stir the pasta into the boiling water and leave to cook according to the packet instructions until al dente. Drain and set aside.

Heat the butter in a frying pan over a medium heat and add a handful of spinach and the nutmeg. Cook the spinach, turning continuously, until wilted then add the remaining spinach, a handful at a time, and cook until wilted.

Finely chop the cooked spinach and add it to the pan with the tomato sauce. Crumble over the ricotta and stir in the pasta. Mix well to combine and serve with the Parmesan.

CRAB CAKES WITH LIME AND TOMATO GUACAMOLE

If you have the time, once you have shaped your crab cakes allow them 30 minutes in the fridge to set. They freeze extremely well. A perfect summer lunch dish, served with a big green salad.

Makes 4 cakes

2 slices of good-quality bread, made into rough breadcrumbs

400g white crab meat

2 tablespoons mayonnaise

drop of Worcestershire sauce

1 tablespoon olive oil

1 dessertspoon finely chopped dill

juice and zest of 1 lemon

butter, for frying

sea salt and freshly ground black pepper

Put all the ingredients, except the butter, in a bowl and season to taste with salt and pepper. Mix well and form the crab mixture into 4 round patties.

Put a frying or griddle pan over a medium heat and add the butter. When the butter begins to foam add the crab cakes and cook for 3 minutes. Turn them over and cook for a further 2 minutes. They should be golden in colour.

Serve with Lime Guacamole.

For the Lime Guacamole

1 ripe avocado

1 ripe plum tomato

1 garlic clove, crushed

2 tablespoons freshly squeezed lime juice

1 tablespoon extra virgin olive oil

1 tablespoon chopped fresh coriander

sea salt and freshly ground black pepper

Cut the avocado in half and discard the stone. Scoop out the flesh and cut it into small cubes. Chop the plum tomatoes into similar sized cubes.

Put the tomato and avocado in a bowl, mix in the garlic, lime juice, olive oil and coriander and mix together well. Season to taste with salt and pepper. Cover with clingfilm immediately because the avocado will quickly discolour.

TIP

To keep your guacamole nice and green, place the avocado stone on top of the dip and cover with clingfilm before chilling.

SCOTCH EGGS

This year was the first time that I made Scotch eggs, and I am now a lifetime member of the Scotch egg fan club! They do take a bit of time to make but they are so worth it.

Makes 4

4 eggs
240g sausagemeat
1 teaspoon finely chopped thyme leaves
1 tablespoon finely chopped flatleaf parsley
1 teaspoon Dijon mustard
zest of 1 lemon
1 spring onion, finely chopped
1 egg, beaten
120g plain flour
120g very fine breadcrumbs
rape seed or sunflower oil, for shallow frying
sea salt and freshly ground black pepper

Put the eggs in a pan of cold water over a high heat and bring to the boil. Reduce the heat and simmer for exactly 7 minutes. Drain and cool the eggs under cold running water, then remove the shells.

Put the sausagemeat in a large mixing bowl with the thyme, parsley, mustard, lemon zest and spring onion. Season with salt and pepper and mix well together until the ingredients are combined.

Dust your hands with flour and take a quarter of the sausage mixture at a time. Roll the meat into a ball and put it on a piece of clingfilm and press slightly. Cover with another sheet of clingfilm and gently roll out into a circle about 5cm across.

Remove the top sheet of clingfilm and put a boiled egg in the centre of the sausage mixture circle. Close the sausage mixture around the egg using the clingfilm underneath as an aid and reshape until you have the perfect egg shape. Remove all the clingfilm. Repeat with the remaining eggs and sausage mixture.

Put the beaten egg in one bowl and the breadcrumbs in another bowl. Dip each Scotch egg into the beaten egg, then roll it in the breadcrumbs.

Put a shallow pan over a medium heat and pour in the oil until it is about two-thirds full. When it is hot carefully drop in the Scotch eggs and fry them for 10 minutes, turning every few minutes to make sure they are evenly fried. Remove from the oil and drain on kitchen paper. Serve at room temperature.

Serves 2

500g butter
1 teaspoon cayenne pepper
500g brown shrimps

POTTED SHRIMP

There is something wonderfully decadent about opening a
Kilner jar of potted shrimp at a picnic and scooping it
on to crispy Melba toast or crackers. They will last for
up to 2 weeks in the fridge.

Clarify the butter by gently melting it in a saucepan. Once the butter
has melted leave it to sit for about 4 minutes to separate. Skim off
the foam that rises to the top and gently pour or spoon the clear
butter off the top, leaving behind the milk solids, which will be at
the bottom of the pan. The clear butter is the clarified butter. Mix
the cayenne pepper with the clarified butter.

Cook the shrimps by placing them in a saucepan of boiling water and
simmering for 5 minutes. The shrimps will turn pink when they are
cooked. Drain and shell the shrimps, by twisting the head to remove it
and pulling off the legs. Hold the tail and pull off the remaining
shell off.

Put the shelled shrimps in a sterilised jar and pour the clarified
butter on top, making sure that the shrimps are completely covered.
Leave to set in the fridge for 1 hour.

SMOKED SALMON PATE

This takes minutes to make, but you do need a good quality smoked salmon. Spread on brown soda bread, toast or crackers.

Serves 6

250g smoked salmon
100g cream cheese
50ml crème fraîche
juice and zest of 1 lemon
1 teaspoon capers
freshly ground black pepper

Put all the ingredients except the pepper into a food-processor and whizz until smooth. Season with pepper to taste.

Transfer to a bowl and chill.

SESAME AND FENNEL MINI SAUSAGE ROLLS

These freeze extremely well and are delicious served with piccalilli or my House Chutney (see page 212).

Makes 20

400g sausagemeat or sausages
2 tablespoons chopped flatleaf parsley
375g sheet of ready-rolled puff pastry
1 beaten egg, to glaze
1 tablespoon fennel seeds
1 tablespoon sesame seeds
sea salt and freshly ground black pepper

Preheat the oven to 180°C/gas mark 4. Put the sausagemeat and flatleaf parsley into a mixing bowl, season with salt and pepper and stir well. Set aside.

Unroll the pastry on to a lightly floured surface and cut it in half lengthways. Divide the sausage mixture in two and spread it along the length of each pastry strip in a cylindrical shape, leaving a 1cm edge.

Tightly roll the pastry around the sausagemeat and brush the ends with the beaten egg to secure. Use a sharp knife to cut each roll into 10 pieces, each about 2.5cm long, and put on a baking tray. Brush more egg all over the pastry and sprinkle the fennel and sesame seeds on top of the sausage rolls.

Cook in the oven for 25-35 minutes until the pastry is puffed and crisp and the meat is cooked through.

PIMM'S

I love to go racing and a trip to the racecourse wouldn't be right without a glass of chilled Pimm's!

Serves 6

200ml Pimm's No. 1
600ml lemonade
1/2 cucumber, sliced
6 strawberries, hulled and halved
1 lemon, cut into wedges
1 orange, cut into wedges
ice

Put all the ingredients in a punch bowl or large jug and mix well.

LEMON SHORTBREAD

You can make lots of variations of this recipe. Try replacing the lemon zest with with orange zest or finely chopped pine nuts.

Makes 10–12

220g butter, softened
110g caster sugar
zest of 1 lemon
1/2 teaspoon vanilla extract
370g plain flour, sifted, plus extra for dusting

Preheat the oven to 160°C/gas mark 3. Line a baking tray with baking parchment.

Cream the butter and sugar together in a large bowl. Add the lemon zest and vanilla extract and blend well. Stir in the flour a little at a time. The dough will be crumbly, so tip it out on to a lightly floured surface and work it together by hand until smooth. Pat or roll out the dough to a rectangle about 1cm thick. Cut into small squares, rectangles or diamonds, whichever you prefer.

Arrange the biscuits on the baking tray and bake in the oven for 20-25 minutes until the edges are just starting to brown.

SPARKING SUMMER BERRY JELLIES

Prosecco adds a lovely sparkle to this summer berry jelly, but for a non-alcoholic version you can just use water instead.

Makes 6

300ml boiling water
55g caster sugar
6 mint or sweet geranium leaves
500ml prosecco (or sparkling wine)
4 leaves of gelatine
200g mixed summer berries (such as raspberries, blueberries and quartered strawberries)

First make a sugar syrup. Put the hot water and sugar in a small saucepan over a low to medium heat, stirring until all the sugar is dissolved, then increase the heat and bring to the boil. Turn down the heat, add the mint or sweet geranium leaves and simmer for 4 minutes.

Pour the wine into a large bowl and add the gelatine. Leave for about 5 minutes or until the gelatine leaves are soft. Using a fork, remove the leaves, squeeze off as much liquid as possible and add the leaves to the sugar syrup. Whisk the syrup until the gelatine has completely dissolved, then pour the syrup back into the bowl with the sparkling wine and whisk to combine. Remove the mint leaves, leave to cool completely, then refrigerate the jelly for about 1 hour.

As soon as the jelly starts to thicken, stir in the summer berries. Divide the jelly between 6 glasses and refrigerate for 4 hours or until they have completely set.

KIDS' LEMONADE ICE LOLLIES

4 lemons
2 oranges
1.5 litres water

For the stock syrup

300g sugar
400ml water
5 sweet geranium leaves

First make the stock syrup. Dissolve the sugar in the water over a gentle heat. Add the geranium leaves and bring to the boil. Boil for 2 minutes then allow to cool.

Juice the fruit and mix well with the stock syrup, adding water to taste. Pour the mixture into popsicle containers and freeze for 1 hour.

WHITE CHOCOLATE AND PASSION FRUIT CHEESECAKE

Sumptuous and creamy, this is one of my favourite desserts to eat in the summer. The hazelnuts in the base add a lovely crunch to the cake. It will last for about five days stored in the fridge.

Makes 1 cake (serves 10)

250g digestive biscuits
50g hazelnuts
180g butter, melted
250g ricotta
250g cream cheese, softened
150g white chocolate, chopped
110g caster sugar
zest of 1 lemon
3 eggs
180ml passion fruit pulp (from about 12 passion fruit)

Preheat the oven to 180°C/gas mark 4. Lightly grease a 23cm springform cake or tart tin.

Put the biscuits and hazelnuts in a food-processor and process until they resemble fine breadcrumbs. Add the butter and mix to combine. Press the mixture into the cake or tart tin and refrigerate for 30 minutes or until firm and cold.

Put the ricotta, cream cheese, white chocolate, caster sugar and lemon zest in the bowl of a food-processor and process until smooth. Gradually add the eggs, processing well after each addition. Fold through the passion fruit pulp and pour the mixture over the base. Bake for 30-35 minutes or until set and allow to cool completely before serving.

MINI VICTORIA SPONGES

These are the cutest little cakes in the world! They are so simple to make yet look and taste divine.

Makes 6

80g unsalted butter, softened, plus extra for greasing

180g caster sugar

3 medium eggs

1 teaspoon vanilla extract

180g self-raising flour, sifted

1 teaspoon baking powder, sifted

icing sugar, for dusting

For the filling

284ml whipping cream

50g icing sugar plus extra for dusting

340g jar strawberry jam

Preheat the oven to 180°C/gas mark 4. Butter and lightly dust six individual tins, each about 7.5cm across and 5.5cm high, with flour.

Put the butter in a large mixing bowl with the sugar and beat together with an electric whisk until light and fluffy.

Slowly beat in the eggs, one at a time, followed by the vanilla extract. When the eggs are fully incorporated, fold in the flour and baking powder.

Spoon the cake mixture evenly into the baking tins and tap the sides to release any air bubbles. Bake in the oven for 20 minutes or until the sponges are lightly golden brown. Check by inserting a skewer into the middle of the cake; if it comes out clean the cake is cooked. Remove from the oven and allow to cool in the tins for about 15 minutes before removing them from the tins and transferring them to a wire rack to cool completely.

Meanwhile, lightly whip the cream and icing sugar together until lightly and fluffy. Cut the cooled sponges in half horizontally through the centre, then spread a generous amount of strawberry jam on the top of the bottom halves, followed by the whipped cream. Put the top halves of the sponges on top and lightly dust with icing sugar.

gourmet mini burgers

JULY

BARBECUE TIME!

I have a photo of my 10 year old self in flowery wellies, standing next to a barbecue, rain dripping off my hood. In my hand is a white bun, a blackened sausage poking out the end. I am wearing a huge grin, smeared in tomato sauce. We often had to bolt from the rain and the sausages, burgers and chicken drumsticks were always incinerated (to avoid food poisoning). But to my 10-year-old palate they were totally delicious.

A foreign exchange visit to stay with the Famille Ronsin in Chateaubourg in France changed everything. Madame Ronsin was a fabulous cook who loved to barbecue. She served barbecued meat, medium rare. It was delicious and no-one died from eating it. At the seaside we had barbecued squid with chilli and crunchy sea salt, gigantic prawns with olive oil and parsley. But the thing I couldn't wait to tell my mum - she barbecued vegetables! Tomatoes, asparagus, mushrooms the size of umbrellas; even green beans were lightly charred and tossed in olive oil. And fruit: peaches, threaded with a rosemary stem, splashed with Marsala, charred and served with a dollop of mascarpone.

The secret to M. Ronsin's elegant, relaxed barbecues was to prepare ahead and keep it simple. Marinade the meat and fish the night before, get the kids to make three fresh salads, *et voila*, ready to roll.

What I learned from my childhood barbecues in Cork and from M. Ronsin, is that barbecue is an attitude. Be creative, try something new but don't get too complicated. Focus on what really matters, fun; enjoying good food with great friends in a relaxed, informal atmosphere.

MEAT

In my early twenties I worked at the White Dog, Nantucket Island, USA for a summer while I was at university. I was working flat out with a mainly Irish staff. At elevenish we'd knock off, grab some burgers and steaks from the kitchen and head for the beach. By the light of car headlamps we'd fire up a barbecue, plonk an old boombox on a rock and dance like madmen. When the coals were hot we'd barbecue the steaks and burgers and eat like it was our last meal on earth.

The great thing with barbecue is, being outside, you can get really smoky. The smoke not only adds great flavour to the meat but also helps cook it. Remember to sear the meat over the hottest part of the barbecue then move the coals to the side so that it can slow-cook over a lower heat. This allows the meat to retain more moisture.

I've included a couple of recipes for rubs and marinades in this chapter but I really encourage you to experiment and create your own. Most of us have all the spices we need for a good rub, hiding away in our kitchen cupboards. Make sure you rub the spices in thoroughly and give the meat time to absorb the flavour. If I'm using a marinade I like to leave it overnight in the fridge.

All the barbecue gadgetry and gourmet recipes can make it seem a little stressful. In fact barbecuing is essentially the simplest form of cooking; perfect for nervous or novice cooks. So get out there and have a go.

FISH

The best barbecued squid I ever had was in Greece.
My friend and I took the ferry to the island of
Alonissos, following the local fishing boats into
harbour. After touring round on a couple of
battered old Vespas, looking for a room to let, I
was starving. Right on cue the wonderful singed,
briny smell of grilled squid wafted in the bedroom
window. We followed our noses down on to the street
and bought a plateful from the vendor. It was
served with just a squeeze of lemon and a sprinkle
of salt and it tasted like heaven. My mouth is
watering just remembering it. It was the freshness
of the squid that was so good, straight off the
fishing boats we docked with. That is the key to a
great fish barbecue — freshness.

When I lived in West Cork I used to go fishing,
usually the catch was mackerel or pollock, both
sustainable. I'd take my fish straight to shore fillet
it and cook it on a little disposable barbecue, you
can get them for next to nothing. I have never had
fish in a restaurant that tasted as good as the fish I
ate on that West Cork beach! The less time the fish
spends between leaving the sea and reaching your
plate the more sensational the taste.

If you can't go fishing yourself (and I do recommend
it), find a good fishmonger. Don't be afraid to ask
what's fresh in that day. The fish eyes should be
bright, the skin should shine and most importantly
it should smell like fresh sea water.

ASIAN MARINADE

Makes approximately 250ml

125ml sunflower oil

75ml rice-wine vinegar

3 tablespoons soy sauce

3 tablespoons chopped fresh ginger

2 tablespoons sugar

Whisk the ingredients together in a bowl. Great with white fish.

INDIAN MARINADE

Makes approximately 200ml

125ml yogurt

2 tablespoons sunflower oil

1 teaspoon ground cumin

1 teaspoon ground turmeric

$\frac{1}{2}$ teaspoon ground coriander

1 tablespoon chopped fresh coriander

Whisk the ingredients together in a bowl. This is perfect for lamb and chicken.

SPICY MARINADE

Makes approximately 185ml

125ml olive oil

2 tablespoons lemon juice

2 tablespoons Dijon mustard

$\frac{1}{2}$ teaspoon crushed dried chilli flakes

Whisk the ingredients together in a bowl. Works well with beef and pork.

juice and zest of 1 lime
1 small red chilli, finely chopped
50ml extra virgin olive oil
16 medium-sized shrimps, shelled and
deveined
1 teaspoon of Dijon mustard
200g rocket leaves
1 avocado, peeled and diced
1 large ripe mango, peeled and diced
sea salt and freshly ground black pepper

SUMMER GRILLED SHRIMP, AVOCADO AND MANGO SALAD

Grab a bag of fresh shrimp, put together the marinade, get the salad ready and fire up the barbecue!

To make the marinade, mix together half the lime juice and zest, the chilli and half the olive oil. Season with salt and pepper and add the shrimps, tossing them to coat completely. Leave to marinate for 15 minutes.

If you are using bamboo skewers, now is the time to soak them in water for 15 minutes so that they do not burn while the food cooks. Thread the marinated shrimps on to the skewers.

Heat the barbecue or grill to medium, or put a frying pan or griddle pan over a medium heat. Grill or fry the shrimps for about 1 minute each side until they are pink and cooked through. Set aside and keep warm.

To make the salad dressing, whisk the Dijon mustard with the remaining lime juice and zest and olive oil. Season with salt and pepper. Arrange the rocket, avocado and mango on a serving plate, place the shrimp skewers on top, drizzle with the dressing and serve.

ITALIAN ORZO PASTA SALAD

If you can't get your hands on orzo pasta, which is a tiny pasta shaped like rice, you can substitute it with penne pasta. It will last for approximately 3 days in the fridge.

Serves 4

250g orzo
2 tablespoons balsamic vinegar
4 tablespoons extra virgin olive oil
1 garlic clove, crushed
¼ red onion, finely diced
12 sun-blushed tomatoes, finely chopped
4 Kalamata olives, pitted and sliced
a small bunch fresh basil, leaves torn
2 tablespoons pine nuts, toasted
sea salt and freshly ground black pepper

First cook the orzo. Fill a large saucepan with salted water, bring to the boil, add the orzo and cook for 8-10 minutes until tender. Drain.

While still hot, toss the orzo in a bowl with the balsamic vinegar, olive oil and garlic. Season to taste with salt and pepper.

Allow the orzo to cool and then mix in a large serving bowl with the onion, sun-blushed tomatoes, olives, basil and pine nuts. Serve immediately.

GREEK SALAD

I often substitute the feta for my local feta-style cheese, which is called Knocklara. It's so creamy and crumbly, much better than the highly processed feta that you find in some supermarkets.

Serves 4

4 tablespoons extra virgin olive oil

2 tablespoons lemon juice

1 garlic clove, crushed

1 teaspoon dried oregano

12 cherry tomatoes, halved

1 cucumber, chopped

200g feta cheese, crumbled with a fork

½ red onion, thinly sliced

8 Kalamata olives, pitted and sliced

leaves from a sprig of mint, finely chopped

sea salt and freshly ground black pepper

First make the dressing. Place the olive oil, lemon juice, crushed garlic and dried oregano in a small bowl, season with salt and pepper and whisk to combine.

Put the remaining ingredients in a large mixing bowl and pour the dressing over them. Toss well and serve.

SICILIAN HUMMUS

Serves 4

400g can chickpeas, rinsed and
drained
about 30 basil leaves
1 garlic clove, crushed
50g almonds
50g pine nuts
zest and juice of 1 lemon
200ml olive oil

Put the chickpeas in a food-
processor and add the remaining
ingredients. Whizz to give a
smooth consistency. The hummus
will last in the fridge for up
to 5 days.

TOMATO SALSA

Serves 4

4 very ripe tomatoes, finely chopped
1 small red onion, finely chopped
2 tablespoons finely chopped fresh
coriander
1 tablespoon extra virgin olive
oil
1 dessertspoon balsamic vinegar
sea salt and freshly ground black
pepper

Put the tomatoes, onion,
coriander, oil and vinegar in a
bowl and mix together. Season
to taste with salt and pepper.

TZATZIKI

Serves 4

300ml natural yogurt
$\frac{1}{2}$ cucumber, grated
$\frac{1}{2}$ red onion, finely diced
1 tablespoon finely chopped dill
1 tablespoon finely chopped mint

Place all of the ingredients in
a bowl and stir to combine.

Serves 4

2 sprigs of rosemary, chopped
2 garlic cloves, crushed
1 red chilli, finely chopped
100ml olive oil
8 lamb chops
sea salt and freshly ground black pepper

BBQ'ED TUSCAN MARINATED LAMB CHOPS

I first discovered this fabulous marinade at a wedding in Tuscany. I squeezed the recipe out of the cook, now I use it to marinate lamb chops, chicken fillets and meaty fish.

Put the rosemary, garlic and chilli in a bowl and cover with the olive oil. Season with salt and pepper and stir well.

Put the lamb chops in a larger bowl, pour the marinade over and rub the mixture into the meat. Cover and leave to marinate in the fridge for an hour or more if there is time.

Cook on a hot barbecue for 3 minutes on each side or for longer if you prefer the meat well done. Delicious served with my Tzatziki (see page 166).

MINI GOURMET BURGERS

I do love a good burger. These mini burger are great for a barbecue, but if you like yours larger just shape to the desired size. If you are making ahead I would do it the day before, any longer will affect the taste.

Makes 12

750g minced beef
1 red onion, finely chopped
1 tablespoon tomato relish
1 teaspoon mustard
1 teaspoon finely chopped thyme
75g fresh breadcrumbs
12 mini sesame burger buns
sea salt and freshly ground black pepper

For the toppings

cheese
cos lettuce
sliced tomatoes
pickles
red onion rings
mayonnaise

Mix the beef with the red onion, relish, mustard, thyme and breadcrumbs and season with salt and pepper. Mix with your hands and shape into 12 mini burgers. Grill on a hot barbecue for 3-4 minutes on each side.

About a minute before the burger is cooked put a slice of cheese on top, if liked. Sandwich the burgers between the burger buns with whatever toppings you fancy and secure with cocktail sticks.

SPICY LAMB KOFTAS WITH TOMATO SALSA AND TZATZIKI

I love lamb koftas along with a chilled beer on a summer evening. They will set better if you leave them overnight in the fridge. I always try and get the trimmed neck of lamb but good-quality minced lamb works well too.

Serves 4

500g minced lamb
1 tablespoon ground cumin
1 teaspoon ground cinnamon
1 red chilli, finely chopped
2 tablespoons finely chopped fresh coriander
2 garlic cloves, crushed
½ red onion, finely chopped

To serve

Tzatziki and Salsa (see page 166)
4 flour tortilla wraps
salad leaves

To make the lamb koftas, put all the ingredients into a bowl and mix well. Shape into 16 balls (each about the size of a golf ball), cover with clingfilm and place in the fridge to set for 1 hour.

Heat the grill or barbecue to medium. (Alternatively set a frying pan over a medium heat and add 1 tablespoon of olive oil.) Brown the koftas on all sides then allow to cook for a further 6-8 minutes.

While the lamb is cooking make the salsa and tzatziki (see page 166).

You can serve the lamb koftas on large skewers (four koftas per person) on a bed of salad leaves with the salsa and tatziki. Alternatively, you could serve them on flour tortilla wraps, with salsa, tatziki and shredded salad leaves, such as cos lettuce leaves.

Barbecue is an attitude. Focus on what really matters – enjoying good food with great friends.

MARGARITA

Besides an Old Fashioned, this is my favourite cocktail. Make sure you chill your glasses in the freezer for 30 minutes before serving.

Makes 1

salt, for rimming the glass
lots of ice
50ml tequila
30ml freshly squeezed lime juice
15ml Cointreau

Put the salt in a shallow dish. Moisten the rim of a glass with damp kitchen paper and dip it in the salt.

Fill the glass with ice. Add the tequila, lime juice, and Cointreau and stir a few times until chilled. Serve immediately.

Serves 4

50ml maple syrup
1 teaspoon Dijon mustard
50g butter, melted
4 corn on the cob
sea salt and freshly
ground black pepper

MAPLE GLAZED GRILLED CORN ON THE COB

Barbecued corn on the cob is delicious with just a smear of butter and ground pepper, but add my maple glaze to the mix and you've got the sweetest thing.

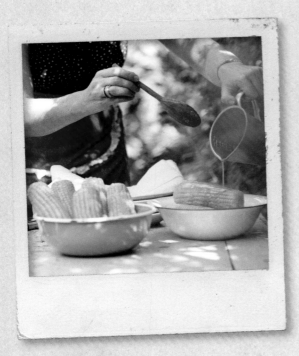

Put the maple syrup, mustard and butter in a bowl and whisk to combine.

Brush the corn on the cob with the glaze and cook on a hot barbecue for about 20 minutes, turning every few minutes.

CELERY, APPLE AND LEMON SLAW

I bet this salad will become a staple at your barbecues, it adds a lovely lightness to grilled meats. It will last for up to 3 days in the fridge.

Serves 6

100ml mayonnaise

2 teaspoons finely chopped flatleaf parsley

juice and zest of 1 lemon

50g freshly grated horseradish

400g celery sticks, halved and cut into strips

4 red apples, cored and cut into strips

1 carrot, halved and cut into strips

sea salt and freshly ground black pepper

Toss all the ingredients together in a large serving bowl and season to taste with salt and pepper. Leave to marinate for an hour before serving.

BARBECUED CHICKEN BURGER

I think fast food joints have done the poor chicken burger no
justice. When homemade using good quality chicken, and
sandwiched in delicious fresh ciabatta baps they are sublime!

Makes 4

600g ground chicken meat
200g fine breadcrumbs
1 onion, finely diced
1 teaspoon Dijon mustard
1 tablespoon lemon juice
4 burger buns
4 slices of Fontina cheese
sea salt and freshly ground
black pepper

To garnish (optional)

sliced tomato
sliced red onion
lettuce
mayonnaise
Dijon mustard
pickles

In a large bowl combine the chicken, breadcrumbs, onion,
mustard and lemon juice. Season to taste with salt and
pepper. Shape into 4 equal patties, each about 175g,
cover and place in the fridge. Refrigerate for about
1 hour.

Grill the chicken burgers on a hot barbecue for 4-5
minutes on each side. Put the cheese on top for the last
minute to melt.

Slice and lightly toast the burger buns, put the patties
in the buns and garnish as liked.

Mini Rosemary
Foccacias

AUGUST

SOUTH OF FRANCE

When I lived in Italy we would drive from Turin down the Cote D'Azur to St Tropez. Sunroof down, scarf tightly tied and huge film-star glasses. It has to be one of the most beautiful drives in the world. Rocky, mountainous coast, cobalt blue sea and drenched in sunshine 300 days a year. For my friend, the drive was the main event. For me, the main attraction was and always will be the food.

The produce is sundrenched and vividly coloured, just like the land it comes from. The herbs are plentiful and so aromatic; rosemary, marjoram, tarragon, thyme and basil. While you may be aware of the fantastic seafood here and the abundance of vegetables, you might be surprised to know the area also produces excellent olives, olive oil and lemons. The region is famous for pistou and passtis. Pistou is a sauce of basil, garlic and olive oil which is often dropped in soups. Passtis is a yellowy aniseed flavoured drink that old men, and sometimes myself, sit and drink in bars. Don't get them mixed up.

This is the kind of food I thrive on. It's so fresh and flavourful. Grilled fish, straight from the sea, and beautiful, colourful, crisp salads with a light olive oil and lemon dressing. With the vitamin D from the sun and all the goodness of the food, I just feel myself getting healthier with every mouthful. Even the tarte au citrone is doing me good, surely?!

ROASTED TOMATO AND BASIL SOUP WITH PARMESAN TOASTS

This soup is similar to an Italian bruschetta topping, in fact that's how I came up with this recipe. I made too much topping and so I turned it into a soup!

Serves 4

800g cherry or plum tomatoes, cut in half

2 garlic cloves, crushed

1 red onion, cut into large chunks

50ml olive oil

1 tablespoon balsamic vinegar

10 basil leaves, torn

500ml hot chicken or vegetable stock

4 slices of baguette

70g grated Parmesan cheese

sea salt and freshly ground black pepper

Preheat the oven to 160°C/gas mark 3.

Put the tomatoes, garlic and onion in a large bowl, pour in the olive oil and vinegar. Season with salt and pepper. Using clean hands, massage the ingredients together for 2 minutes so that the flavours come together. Transfer to a roasting dish and cook in the oven for 20 minutes.

Tip the tomatoes, garlic and onion into a saucepan. Add the basil and stock, set over a low heat and allow to simmer for 15 minutes.

Meanwhile, cover the baguette slices with grated Parmesan and cook in the oven until the cheese has melted. Top each soup bowl with a slice of toast. This soup is also delicious with mini rosemary focaccia (see page 192).

CAMEMBERT AND TOMATO TART

This is a classic in good French cafés and I hope it will become a classic in your kitchen too. Try to make the time to chill the pastry for an hour before you bake as this will make the pastry flakier.

Serves 6

For the pastry

225g plain flour
100g unsalted butter, cut into small cubes
2 tbsps water
pinch of salt

For the filling

80g Gruyère cheese, grated
1 tablespoon Dijon mustard
1 tablespoon chopped thyme leaves
1 garlic clove, crushed
200g camembert cheese, cut into thin strips
10 cherry tomatoes, halved
sea salt and freshly ground black pepper

Make the pastry. Put the butter, flour and salt in a food-processor and blend until the mixture resembles fine breadcrumbs. Pour in the water and mix again until the dough starts to come together, adding more water if necessary.

Tip the pastry on to a lightly floured surface, gather together until smooth, then roll out and line a 23 × 2.5cm loose-bottom fluted flan tin. Trim the edges and press the pastry into flutes. Prick the base with a fork.

Pour baking beans on top of the foil and bake the pastry 'blind' in the oven for 15 minutes. Remove and allow to cool.

Make the filling. In a bowl mix together the Gruyère, mustard, thyme, garlic and season with salt and pepper. Pour the mixture into the pastry case, spreading it out evenly with the back of a spoon. Arrange the strips of camembert and halved tomatoes on top and bake in the oven for 35 minutes. Serve warm.

Serves 4

400g watermelon, chopped and seeds removed
450g plum tomatoes, chopped
large cucumber, diced
1 spring onion, finely sliced
2 tablespoons extra virgin olive oil
1 tablespoon balsamic vinegar
250g feta cheese, crumbled
1 teaspoon dried oregano
sea salt and freshly ground black pepper

SUMMER WATERMELON, FETA AND MINT SALAD

This is so fresh and bursting with summer flavours.
I sometimes replace the watermelon with cantaloupe
melon, or add parma ham and replace the feta with
soft goat's cheese.

Put the watermelon, tomatoes, cucumber and spring
onion in a large serving bowl.

Pour over the oil and balsamic vinegar and season with
salt and pepper. Sprinkle over the oregano and mix
well. Crumble the feta over the salad and serve.

SEARED TUNA NICOISE SALAD

Please don't be tempted to cook the tuna for longer than one minute on each side, it's too beautiful to be over-cooked. This was on the summer menu at Clodagh's Kitchen Restaurant and turned out to be our 2nd best seller!

Serves 2

1 egg, hardboiled and shelled

4 new potatoes, scrubbed, cooked and halved

12 French beans, cooked

120g salad leaves

2 tomatoes, quartered

40ml French dressing

12 black olives

2 fresh tuna steaks

20ml olive oil

sea salt and freshly ground black pepper

Cut the egg into quarters and put in a mixing bowl with the potatoes, French beans, salad leaves and tomatoes. Pour in the French dressing and toss well. Divide between two plates and sprinkle the olives on top.

Season the tuna steaks with salt and pepper. Put a frying pan over a high heat, add the oil and sear the tuna on both sides for 1 minute. Take care that you do not cook the tuna for longer than 1 minute on each side or it will taste like chicken. Put a tuna steak onto each plate and serve

PAN-ROASTED JOHN DORY WITH MINTED BEURRE BLANC

John Dory is one of my favourite fish, grilled or roasted. I particularly love to serve it with my minted beurre blanc and some spinach and new potatoes.

Serves 4

2 tablespoons butter
8 small fillets of John Dory
juice of 1 lemon
sea salt and freshly ground black pepper

For the beurre blanc

2 shallots, finely sliced
2 tablespoons white wine vinegar
6 tablespoons Muscadet
2 tablespoons cream
150g unsalted butter, diced
juice of 1 lemon
1 tablespoon chopped mint leaves

To make the beurre blanc, place the shallots, vinegar and wine in a pan and reduce until there is almost no liquid left. Stir in the cream and heat gently. Whisk in the butter a little at a time, never allowing the sauce to boil. Season with lemon juice and a little salt and black pepper and stir in the fresh mint.

Now cook the John Dory. Place a frying pan over a medium heat and melt the butter. Once the butter is melted, place the fish in the pan skin down and season with salt and pepper. Leave to cook for 3 minutes, then turn and cook for a further 4 minutes. Squeeze the juice of 1 lemon over the fish once you have turned it and chop up the lemon skin and tuck around the dish to add more flavor.

Serve the fish with a drizzle of the minted beurre blanc, buttered spinach and new potatoes.

MINI ROSEMARY FOCCACIAS

Once you get the hang of the method there are endless variations you can make, such as sun-blushed tomatoes and basil, olive and oregano or caramelised red onion and feta.

Makes 4

1 teaspoon fresh yeast
1 teaspoon sugar
70ml warm water
125g strong white flour
1 teaspoon table salt
olive oil
sea salt, for sprinkling
1 tablespoon finely chopped rosemary

Preheat the oven to 200°C/gas mark 6. Line a baking tray with greaseproof paper.

Put the yeast and sugar in a small bowl and, using the back of a teaspoon, rub the sugar into the yeast until it turns to liquid. Whisk in the water and continue to whisk for about 2 minutes or until you get a frothy top.

Put the flour in a large bowl and stir in the salt. Make a well in the centre and use a wooden spoon to stir in the liquid.

Lightly oil your working surface and turn out the dough. Knead it about 20 times until you have a soft dough. Return it to the bowl and, using your hands, cover it with oil. Cover the bowl with a tea-towel and put it in a warm place (such as an airing cupboard). After 1 hour turn it back out on to an oiled surface and knead again 20 times, returning it to the airing cupboard for another hour.

Turn the dough on to an oiled surface again and cut it into four balls. Oil a wooden rolling pin and roll the balls into small loaves, 10-12cm across. Put them on the baking tray and use your fingers to make little indentations over the surface. Sprinkle over the finely chopped rosemary and sea salt and cook in the oven for 20 minutes.

OLIVE CRISP BREADS

This is my stand-by bread recipe when I have people coming for dinner. I love placing them on my guests napkins as they look so colourful.

Makes 8

125ml warm water
1 teaspoon dry fast-action yeast
210g plain flour
2 tablespoons olive oil
100g Kalamata olives, pitted and finely chopped
sea salt

Preheat the oven to 180°C/gas mark 4. Line two baking trays with greaseproof paper.

Pour the water in a bowl and sprinkle in the yeast. Whisk well and allow the yeast to foam, which should take about 5 minutes.

Sift the flour into a large bowl and make a well in the centre. Pour in two-thirds of the yeast mixture and add the oil and a sprinkle of sea salt. Stir together until a dough forms, adding more of the yeast mixture if needed. The dough should be moist but not sticky.

Tip the dough on to a floured surface and knead for 10 minutes. Transfer to an oiled bowl, cover with a tea-towel or clingfilm and put in a warm, dry place, such as an airing cupboard, for an hour.

Divide the dough into eight pieces and on a lightly floured surface roll out each piece to about 24 × 10cm. Transfer to the baking tray, brush with olive oil and sprinkle the finely chopped olives on top, using the back of a spoon to push the olives gently into the dough. Bake in the oven for 15 minutes or until crisp and golden. Leave to cool on wire racks before serving.

VARIATIONS

There are so many variations that can be made with the crisps breads. Try any of the following combinations:
• Finely chopped pine nuts.
• Rosemary and sea salt.
• Finely chopped sun blushed tomatoes and dried oregano.

HOMEMADE PIZZA

I make fresh pizza for two reasons; firstly because it tastes so good, and second, at the risk of sounding hippy dippy, I find it therapeutic. Use my fresh tomato pizza base and then top with whatever your heart or tummy desires!

Makes 2 x 30cm pizzas

5g fresh yeast
1 teaspoon caster sugar
50ml warm water
350g strong white flour
1 teaspoon salt
1 tablespoon olive oil, plus extra for brushing

Preheat the oven to 230°C/gas mark 8.

Put the yeast and sugar in a small bowl and use the back of a teaspoon to rub the sugar into the yeast until it turns to liquid. Whisk in the warm water and continue to whisk for about 2 minutes or until frothy.

Sift the flour into a large bowl and mix in the salt. Make a well in the centre of the flour and pour in two-thirds of the yeast into the well of the flour and mix together to give a soft, but not sticky dough. Add the olive oil and mix well, add extra oil to the dough if needed.

Take the dough out of the bowl. Knead it on a lightly floured worktop for 10 minutes or until it feels smooth and slightly springy. (If you do this in a food mixer with the dough hook it takes half the time.) Let the dough relax for a few minutes.

Shape the dough into two equal balls. Lightly brush the balls with oil, cover and leave to prove in a warm place, such as an airing cupboard, for 1 hour.

Put a flat sheet or an upside down baking tray in the oven. (It's easier to slide the pizza on and off if the surface does not have a lip.) On a lightly floured work surface roll out each ball of dough to a circle about 30cm across.

Put a pizza base on a second, cool, upside-down floured tray, spread with Roasted Tomato, Basil and Olive Sauce (see page 193) and sprinkle with your chosen toppings.

Slide the pizza off the cool tray on to the hot tray in the centre of the oven and cook for 5-10 minutes, depending on the heat of the oven and the thickness of the pizza, until the pizza is golden underneath and bubbling on top.

ROASTED TOMATO, BASIL AND OLIVE SAUCE

This is one of my classic recipes that I use over and over again. You are going to love it, I know you will. Excuse me for sounding confident but it is a great recipe!

Serves 4 for pasta or enough for 2 pizza bases (see page 194)

300g ripe plum tomatoes, halved

1 onion, finely chopped

2 garlic cloves, crushed

20 black olives, pitted and halved

20 basil leaves

2 tablespoons olive oil

sea salt and freshly ground black pepper

Preheat the oven to 180°C/gas mark 4.

Put the tomatoes, cut side up, in a roasting tin. Sprinkle over the onion, garlic, olives, basil and oil and season with salt and pepper. Cook in the oven for 15 minutes or until the tomatoes have roasted.

When the tomatoes are cooked transfer the contents of the roasting tin to a food-processor and blend to make a smooth sauce.

SPINACH, RICOTTA AND TOMATO CALZONE

Oooohhh calzones, I love you too much! Really I think I love them more then pizza. I think of them as the Italian pie. You can add pancetta or mushrooms to this recipe too.

Makes 2 calzones

pizza dough (see page 194)

1 tablespoon olive oil, plus extra for brushing

200g baby spinach

1 garlic clove, crushed

100ml tomato sauce

150g ricotta

70g Parmesan cheese, grated

sea salt and freshly ground black pepper

Preheat the oven to 220°C/gas mark 7. Flour a baking tray.

Make the pizza dough and roll out two circles, each about 30cm across.

Make the filling. Heat the oil in a hot frying pan, add the spinach and toss it briefly in the oil. Add the garlic and continue to cook until the spinach is wilted. Stir in the tomato sauce, ricotta and Parmesan and season with salt and pepper. Remove from the heat and allow to cool. Take care that the filling isn't too runny, or it will burst through the dough when you cook the calzones, you can thicken with some flour or cornflour if the filling seems too runny.

Divide the filling evenly between the pizza bases and spread it out. Carefully lift the far edge of the dough circle and pull it over the filling towards you. You should be aiming to fold it in half so that it resembles a large Cornish pasty. Brush the edges with olive oil and crimp them so that none of the filling can spill out. Cut a few slashes in the dough. Put the calzones side by side on the baking tray (use two if necessary). You could also use a pizza stone or granite slab. Cook at the bottom of the oven for 10-15 minutes or until the dough is puffed up and golden on top, and the filling is hot.

LEMON DRIZZLE CAKE

This is how a lemon drizzle cake should be; light, fluffy, zesty and made sweet by the drizzle. It will last about 5 days in an airtight container.

Serves 8-10
For the cake

225g butter, softened
225g caster sugar
3 eggs
275g self-raising flour, sifted
2 teaspoon baking powder, sifted
zest of 2 lemons, plus extra to decorate
juice of 1 lemon
2 tablespoons milk
lemon slices, to decorate

For the drizzle

juice of 2 lemons
175g icing sugar

Preheat the oven to 180°C/gas mark 4. Grease a 20-22cm round cake tin and line the base with baking parchment.

Put the butter in a large mixing bowl with the sugar and beat together with a whisk until light and fluffy.

Slowly beat in the eggs, one at a time. When the eggs are fully incorporated add the milk, then fold in the flour, baking powder and lemon zest. Pour the cake mixture into the tin and tap the sides to release any air bubbles. Bake in the oven for 35-40 minutes or until the sponge is lightly golden brown. Check by inserting a skewer into the centre of the cake; if it comes out clean the cake is cooked.

While the cake is still hot and still in the tin prick it with a skewer or tooth pick and pour over the lemon juice. Leave the cake in the tin to cool.

Make the drizzle. Mix the lemon juice, a little at a time, into the icing sugar to make a smooth paste. Remove the cake from the tin and smooth the icing over the top. Decorate with slices of lemon and extra lemon zest.

HOMEMADE STRAWBERRY ICE CREAM

If you don't have an ice cream maker, freeze once the mixture is made and remove every 30 minutes, whisk and return to the freezer again.

Serves 8

4 egg yolks
125g caster sugar
150ml milk
500ml double cream
vanilla pod, or few drops vanilla extract
400g strawberries, hulled and roughly chopped

Put the egg yolks in a large bowl and add 75g caster sugar. Whisk until light, fluffy and pale in colour.

Put the milk, half the cream and vanilla seeds or extract in a saucepan and bring to the boil. Watch the pan carefully to make sure it does not overflow. Pour the boiling milk mixture over the whisked egg yolks, whisking all the time to make sure that the eggs do not cook or scramble. Add the remainder of the cream into the bowl and stir. Leave to cool.

In another bowl mix the strawberries with the remaining caster sugar. Mash the strawberries with a fork until they make a thick sauce. Add to the cooled egg mixture and stir well.

Put the mixture into a clean bowl or container and transfer to the freezer.

After 30 minutes take the bowl from the freezer and whisk to remove any crystals that have formed. Return to the freezer and repeat the whisking process until the ice cream is set. Alternatively, if you have an ice-cream maker, churn the ice cream, transfer it to a container and freeze until it is ready to eat.

EASY SUMMER ICE CREAM CAKE

I sometimes freeze this in a round cake tin so it looks like a proper cake and then sprinkle chocolates curls all over. It will be one of the quickest cakes you ever make.

Serves 6

300ml whipping cream
8 x 8cm meringue nests
300g summer berries
2 teaspoons caster sugar
1/2 teaspoon vanilla extract
1 teaspoon mint leaves, finely chopped

Line a 450g loaf or cake tin with clingfilm.

Whip the cream in a bowl. Break up the meringue nests. In a separate bowl use a fork to mash the summer berries with the sugar.

Fold the mashed berries, vanilla extract and mint into the whipped cream. Stir in the crushed meringues.

Tip in the berry and meringue mixture into the cake tin, cover with more clingfilm and put in the freezer for 2-3 hours or until frozen.

Take the cake from the freezer just before serving. Remove the clingfilm from the top, turn the tin over on to a plate or board and remove the rest of the clingfilm. Serve the cake in slices.

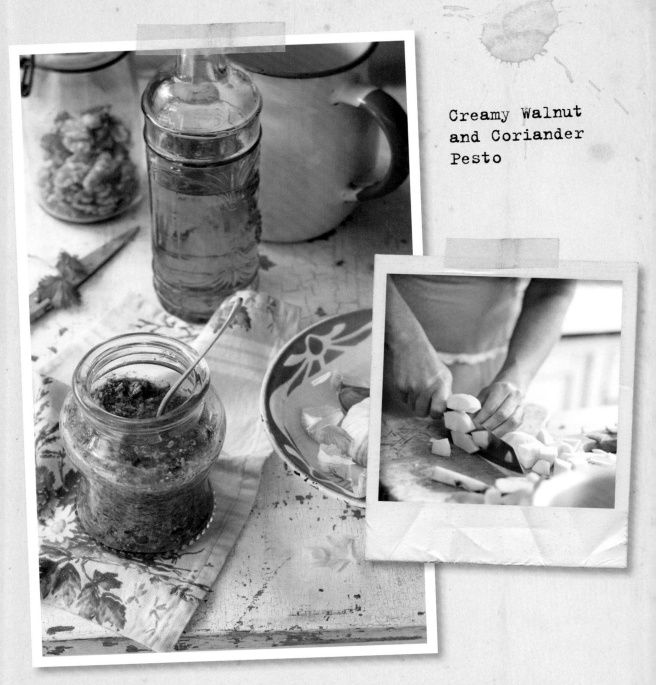

Creamy Walnut
and Coriander
Pesto

SEPTEMBER

SEPTEMBER PRESERVING PARTY!

Last autumn I had an abundance of gorgeous harvest produce. I had a crate of plump, peppery-smelling tomatoes from a friend's allotment, baskets of native Irish apples, a tub of blackberries I picked with my nieces and armfuls of my homegrown rocket that needed using immediately. Now I know preserving is important and a great way of passing on granny skills but I just wasn't feeling very motivated. Then I had an idea - why not make a necessary and important task into a fun day event for friends? A Preserving Party.

Organisation was minimal. I sent a recipe out to each of four friends. On the day I divided the big island in the centre of my kitchen into sections, each with its own chopping board and recipe taped on the work surface next to it. I made a big bowl of pasta for lunch and bought in a few bottles of wine. On the morning I sterilised jars and got the labels ready. And that was it.

As soon as my friends arrived we got stuck in, chopping, chatting and cooking. The smells were tantalising, a cross between a souk and a food hall at Christmas. When you're having that much fun you're not aware of how hard you're working. We were astonished when the jars were all filled by lunchtime. Over pasta we kept glancing over at our handiwork with that deep satisfaction you get when you've been really industrious.

At the end of the day we had a sampling session. I brought crackers, cheese and some pâté to accompany the tomato chutney, walnut and rocket pesto, berry jam and vanilla and fig compote. I ran out of adjectives and just started groaning with pleasure. Everyone went home not just with a box full of jars for their store cupboards but a real sense of having spent precious, stolen moments together. We didn't just laugh a lot, we learned a lot. I know it will become an annual tradition and that the five of us will be having preserving parties in our eighties and I can't wait!

STEPS AND TIPS ON PRESERVING

How to test if your jam is cooked

- Place a saucer in a freezer.
- Place a teaspoon of jam on the chilled saucer.
- Drag your finger over the jam.
- If the jam wrinkles then it has set.

How to sterilise your jars

- Preheat the oven to 180°C/gas mark 4.
- Thoroughly wash the jars and lids and place them, upside down, on a baking tray lined with baking parchment.
- Put the jars and lids in the oven for 20 minutes. Remove from the oven and allow to cool.

Tips on preserving

- Only fill each jar to within 50mm of the top.
- If you want to reduce the amount of sugar you use when making jam, substitute half the recommended quantity with honey.
- If the preserve is cooled it should be spooned into a cooled sterilised jar; if the preserve is warm it should be spooned into a warmed sterilised jar.
- When you are bottling non-liquid foods it's important to remove any trapped air bubbles from the top of the jar. Skim the top of the preserve with a knife.

Makes 6 x 240ml jars
500g blackberries
500g cooking apples,
peeled, cored and chopped
100ml water
juice of 1 small lemon
1kg preserving sugar

BLACKBERRY AND APPLE JAM

I have the most wonderful memories of picking blackberries with my siblings as a child, and taking our treasured berries back to our mum who would make blackberry and apple jam. That memory is so precious to me and nothing will keep me from making this jam every year.

Put the blackberries, apples, water and lemon juice into a large saucepan or preserving pan. Set the pan over a medium heat and bring to the boil. Reduce the heat and simmer for 10 minutes.

Stir in the sugar and bring the jam back to the boil. Continue to boil for 5 minutes, stirring until all the sugar has dissolved.

Spoon into sterilised jars (see page 204).

VARIATIONS

Strawberry and Vanilla Jam:
Follow recipe left, omitting the blackberries and apples and replacing with 1kg fresh hulled and quartered strawberries and the seeds from 1 vanilla pod.

Blueberry Jam:
Follow recipe left, omitting the blackberries and apples and replacing with 1kg fresh blueberries left whole.

FIG JAM

I make fig jam for one thing and that's to eat with aged
hard or smoky cheeses, like Pecorino or Coolea, it's a
little piece of heaven for me, along with a glass of
Côtes du Rhône.

Makes 3 x 240ml jars

150ml balsamic vinegar
200ml red wine vinegar
400g soft brown sugar
zest and juice of
1 lemon
1 red onion, diced
1 teaspoon mustard seeds
5cm piece of fresh
ginger, peeled and
grated
1 teaspoon allspice
1 cinnamon stick
1kg (13) fresh figs
sea salt and freshly
ground black pepper

Put a large saucepan or preserving pan over a medium
heat and add the vinegars, sugar, lemon zest and
juice, onion, mustard seeds, ginger, allspice and
cinnamon stick. Season to taste with salt and pepper.
Stir well and bring the boil. Reduce the heat and
simmer for another 15 minutes or until a thick syrup
has formed.

Remove the stems from the figs and cut them in half.
Stir them into the thick syrup and continue to simmer
for a further 20 minutes.

Once the mixture has cooled
spoon it into sterilised jars
(see page 204).

Makes 6 x 230ml jars
1kg (5 large) oranges
1 litre water
juice of 2 lemons
1kg preserving sugar

OLD FASHIONED MARMALADE

Homemade marmalade is delicious smothered over toast with a cup of tea. Is there anything better on a September morning? In September in Italy the markets would be stacked with oranges from Sicily.

Cut the oranges into quarters. Using a sharp knife, carefully cut the flesh away from the rind, taking care to leave all the pith behind. Cut the flesh into thin slices and place them in a bowl.

Use a sharp fruit knife or small knife to scrape off and discard all the membrane and pith from the rind. Cut the rind into thin slivers and put them in a saucepan with the water. Bring to the boil, reduce the heat to a simmer and cook for about 2 hours or until the rinds are tender.

Add the lemon juice to the orange flesh in the bowl and mix. Put the orange flesh in the centre of a square of muslin and gather the sides together like a bag. Tie it at the top. Fasten the bag to the handle of a saucepan and allow the bag to hang inside the pan to collect all the juice. Leave it to drain for a couple of hours.

Squeeze any remaining juices from the muslin bag into the saucepan and discard the bag and its contents. Stir in the sugar and orange rind. Put the saucepan over a low heat and cook, stirring occasionally, for about 15 minutes or until all the sugar has dissolved.

Allow the orange mixture to sit for 10 minutes off the heat, then spoon it into warmed sterilised jars (see page 204). Leave to cool completely and then cover with a lid.

CREAMY WALNUT AND CORIANDER PESTO

Delicious tossed in pasta, drizzled over soft cheeses or as a dip. I sometimes add a little feta into the mix for a salty version that works well with pasta.

Serves 4

110g fresh coriander
150ml extra virgin olive oil
50g walnuts
2 garlic cloves
50g Parmesan cheese, grated
a pinch of sea salt

Put all the ingredients in a food-processor and whizz to give a smooth/coarse texture.

END OF SUMMER TOMATO CHUTNEY

Opening that end of summer burst of flavours in October to spread over a melted cheese toastie is just heaven. The chutney will keep for 3 months in a sterilised jar.

Makes about 3 kg

2kg ripe tomatoes
5cm piece of fresh ginger, peeled and grated
500g apples
200g raisins
2 onions, finely diced
1/2 teaspoon paprika
1 teaspoon chilli powder
2 teaspoons salt
500g brown sugar
600ml cider vinegar

Peel the tomatoes. Cut a cross at the top of each one, put them into a large bowl of boiling water for 5 minutes or until the skins start to crack (this will depend on how ripe the tomatoes are). Transfer to a bowl of cold water and remove the skins.

Put the tomatoes and ginger in a food-processor and blend until smooth.

Set a large saucepan or preserving pan over a medium heat and add the blended tomatoes and ginger. Stir in the remaining ingredients. Bring to the boil, reduce the heat and simmer for about 40 minutes or until the chutney has begun to thicken.

Cool and spoon into sterilised jars (see page 204).

Makes 12 x 230ml jars

2kg cooking apples,
peeled, quartered and
cored

2 onions

50g butter

500g brown sugar

20 cloves

1 tablespoon chilli
powder

1 tablespoon turmeric

10cm piece of fresh
ginger, peeled and grated

400ml cider vinegar

sea salt and freshly
ground black pepper

OUR HOUSE CHUTNEY

This really is the best preserve that I
have made, it lasts for about 3 months
and is even better if left to age for at
least 1 week before you eat.

Chop the apples into small chunks and dice the onions.

Set a large saucepan or preserving pan over a low heat
and melt the butter. Add the apples and onions, then add
the sugar, cloves, chilli powder, turmeric, ginger and
cider vinegar. Season to taste with salt and pepper and
mix well.

Cover the saucepan, increase the heat and bring to the
boil. Reduce the heat and leave to simmer over a medium
heat for 20 minutes, stirring every 5 minutes.

Take off the saucepan lid, turn down the heat and leave
to cook for 30 minutes until the apple has broken down
and the chutney has turned a rich, golden brown colour.
Use the back of a wooden spoon to crush the apples if
necessary. Take the pan off the heat and allow to cool.
The chutney will thicken more as it cools.

Spoon the cool chutney into sterilised jars (see page
204).

LUNCHBOXES

Stolen moments are important. Taking back a little time to do
something good for yourself isn't selfish, it's an investment
in your own well being. It's all too easy to grab a soggy
sandwich at lunchtime and sit at your desk in front of the
computer. With very little pre-planning you could steal back a
few moments to give yourself a real treat.

I have a friend, Tom. When he takes the lid off his packed
lunch he lifts it up, smells it and smiles. He brings his own
cloth napkin to work and a little knife to slice cold meats,
cheese or fruits. He is a connoisseur of the lunchbox and
here's what I learned from him:

Find yourself a little pot (the individual catering jars of
jam and mustard are perfect); use this for your chutneys,
pesto and pickles. If you put them straight into the sandwich
it will be soggy by lunchtime. It doesn't always have to be
bread, mix it up with salads, tortilla or hearty homemade
soups. And finally, always pack yourself a treat. For Tom that
was something home baked and sweet and the envy of all who
worked with him.

Get away from your desk if you can. Go outside, meet a friend
and share your packed lunches, sit by the river. Give yourself
the time to enjoy your food. Let's put the pleasure back into
the packed lunch. Here are some of my recipes for the
delicious sandwiches and salads we make at Clodagh's Bakery
in Dublin.

ITALIAN MINESTRONE SOUP

On the piazza where I lived in Turin, there was a fabulous daily market. I would pop down early in the morning and fill my bag with delicious vegetables to make this soup.

Serves 6

2 tablespoons olive oil

1 onion, finely chopped

2 garlic cloves, crushed

1 carrot, finely chopped

1 celery stick, finely chopped

1 courgette, finely chopped

800ml hot vegetable stock

400g can chopped tomatoes

400g can chickpeas, rinsed and drained

1 teaspoon dried oregano

sea salt and freshly ground black pepper

Put a large saucepan over a medium-high heat, pour in the oil and then stir in the onion and garlic. Cover and allow to cook for 2 minutes.

Stir in the carrot, celery and courgette. Cover and leave to cook for a further 5 minutes.

Pour in the stock, tomatoes and chickpeas. Bring to the boil, reduce the heat and simmer. Stir in the oregano, season with salt and pepper and continue to simmer for about 10 minutes.

CHICKEN CAESAR WRAP

Creamy, crunchy and light – the perfect summer lunch. Try adding a sun-blushed tomato salad with lime dressing.

Makes 2 wraps

1 chicken breast
2 tablespoons Caesar dressing (see page 113)
8 Cos lettuce leaves
2 flour wraps
1 tablespoon pine nuts, toasted and roughly chopped

For the marinade

juice of $\frac{1}{2}$ lemon
1 garlic clove, crushed
1 tablespoon olive oil
sea salt and freshly ground black pepper

Preheat the oven to 180°C/gas mark 4.

Make the marinade. Put the lemon juice, garlic and oil in a bowl or sealable freezer bag and season with salt and pepper. Add the chicken, mix well and leave in the fridge for 30 minutes.

Place a griddle or frying pan over a medium heat and sear the chicken for about 3 minutes on each side or until golden in colour. Transfer to the oven and cook for 10 minutes. Remove and allow to cool.

Cut the chicken into strips, place in a bowl with the Caesar dressing and mix well.

Open out the wraps and place the lettuce in the centre of each. Add the chicken, sprinkle over the chopped pine nuts and fold the wraps to close.

Try adding any of the following:

- Sun-blushed tomatoes
- Croutons
- Crispy bacon lardons

Makes 2

2 Mini Rosemary Focaccias (see page 192)
extra virgin olive oil
1 ball of fresh buffalo mozzarella, sliced
6 sun-blushed tomatoes, roughly chopped
2 slices of prosciutto di Parma (Parma ham)
6 fresh basil leaves, torn
sea salt and freshly ground black pepper

THE ITALIAN JOB

For the cheese, use mozzarella di buffalo — and, as September is the best month for tomatoes, I would use fresh — but once out of season, I'll be using sun-blushed.

Cut the focaccias in half lengthways and brush with oil.

Divide the mozzarella and tomatoes between the focaccias. Add a slice of prosciutto to each and scatter over the basil. Season with salt and pepper and close the sandwich.

TUNA MELT

When you're shopping for tinned tuna, look for the 'sustainably fished' logo. The cucumber adds a gorgeous freshness. You could also toss the filling in salad leaves.

Makes 2

250g can tuna, preferably in oil, drained and flaked
80ml mayonnaise
$\frac{1}{2}$ celery stick, finely sliced
$\frac{1}{4}$ red onion, finely sliced
juice of $\frac{1}{2}$ lemon
2 demi sourdough baguettes
4 slices of tomato
5cm cucumber, finely diced
2 slices of Swiss cheese
sea salt and freshly ground pepper

Preheat the oven to 200°C/gas mark 6.

Put the tuna, mayonnaise, celery, onion and lemon juice in a bowl. Season with salt and pepper and mix well.

Cut the baguettes in half lengthways and divide the tuna mayonnaise between them. Put two slices of tomato in each sandwich, followed by a slice of cheese. Close the baguette together.

Cook in the oven for 5-7 minutes.

Aternatively, cook the sandwich in a griddle or sandwich-maker.

MINI 3 BEAN SALAD

Bursting with fibre, this salad will give you that extra 'oomph' for your afternoon at work. We serve this on the salad counter in the food court. I try and have a portion 3 times a week - so stock up your store cupboard with canned pulses!

Makes 10 mini salads

400g can cannellini beans, rinsed and drained

400g can kidney beans, rinsed and drained

400g can chickpeas, rinsed and drained

1 celery stick, finely sliced

½ red onion, finely diced

3 tablespoons finely chopped flatleaf parsley

1 garlic clove, crushed

1 teaspoon dried oregano

For the vinaigrette:

100ml extra virgin olive oil

70ml cider vinegar

sea salt and freshly ground black pepper

Make the vinaigrette. Whisk together the oil and vinegar and season to taste with salt and pepper.

Put all the ingredients for the salad in a large mixing bowl. Pour the vinaigrette over and mix well. Cover and place in the fridge for an hour before serving

Makes 5 mini salads

50g of flaked almonds
450g carrots
100g golden raisins
1 tablespoon finely chopped flatleaf
parsley

For the vinaigrette:

2 tablespoons extra virgin olive oil
5 tablespoons white wine vinegar
sea salt and freshly ground black
pepper

MINI CARROT, RAISIN AND ALMOND SALAD

Gorgeous alongside a slice of quiche or sandwich and lovely tumbled in with my 3 bean salad. This salad is another staple in my salad bar at Homemade Food Court. Make a big batch and this salad will last up to 4 days in the fridge.

Toast the almonds on a dry baking tray in the oven at 180°C/gas mark 4 for 10 minutes or or in a dry frying pan until golden brown. Set aside to cool.

Peel the carrots and grate them into a large bowl using the large side of the grater. Mix in the raisins and almonds.

Make the vinaigrette. Whisk together the oil and vinegar and season to taste with salt and pepper.

Pour the vinaigrette over the carrots and mix well. Cover and place in the fridge for an hour.

Add the parsley just before serving.

CHICKEN, AVOCADO AND SUN-BLUSHED TOMATO SALAD WITH A LIME DRESSING

The lime dressing in this salad adds a delicious zestiness to the chicken and avocado. Triple the dressing recipe and it will keep in the fridge for up to 2 weeks.

For the Chicken:

juice of ½ lemon
1 garlic clove, crushed
1 tablespoon olive oil
1 skinless chicken breast
sea salt and freshly ground black pepper

For the Salad:

mixed salad leaves
1 avocado, sliced
8 sun-blushed tomatoes
16 pumpkin seeds

For the Dressing:

3 tablespoons extra virgin olive oil
juice of 1 lime

Preheat the oven to 180°C/gas mark 4.

Put the lemon juice, garlic and oil in a bowl or sealable freezer bag and season with salt and pepper. Add the chicken to the marinade and mix well. Put in the fridge for 30 minutes.

Put a griddle or frying pan over a medium heat and sear the chicken for about 3 minutes on each side or until golden in colour. Transfer to the oven for 10 minutes to cook completely. Remove and allow to cool.

Cut the chicken into strips and put them in a bowl. Add the salad leaves, avocado slices, sun-blushed tomatoes and pumpkin seeds.

Make the dressing. Whisk together the oil and lime juice and season with salt and pepper. Pour the dressing over the salad and toss to mix.

VERMICELLI NOODLE SALAD WITH ONION AND SESAME DRESSING

This delicious salad makes a fabulous Eastern inspired lunch. The onion and sesame dressing adds a great flavour to the noodles.

Serves 2

450g mung beans or vermicelli noodles

a handful of seeds (such as pumpkin, sunflower or sesame)

a splash of Kikkoman soy sauce

1 carrot, finely grated

1 beetroot, finely grated

½ daikon (Japanese radish), finely grated (or a white cabbage heart)

2 tablespoons finely chopped fresh coriander

2 tablespoons spring onions, finely chopped

For the Onion & Sesame Dressing:

½ large onion or 1 small onion, diced

100ml Kikkoman soy sauce

100ml sesame oil

80ml rice vinegar

20g caster sugar

sesame seeds, for sprinkling

Preheat the oven to 180°C/gas mark 4.

Make the dressing by putting all the ingredients (except the sesame seeds) in a blender. Mix until smooth, transfer to a bowl and sprinkle the sesame seeds over the top.

Cook the noodles in boiling water for 2-3 minutes or according to the pack instructions. Cool under cold running water and drain well.

Place the seeds on a baking tray, sprinkle over the soy sauce and cook in the oven for 5-7 minutes.

Using your hands, gently mix the noodles with all the other ingredients until you're happy with the blend. Sprinkle the warm seeds on top and serve with the sauce on the side.

HEAVENLY CHOCOLATE BROWNIES

You can substitute the walnuts with hazelnuts or fresh berries such as raspberries. Make a lovely big tray and store them in an airtight container and they will last for up to a week.

Makes 20

230g butter
180g dark chocolate (70 per cent cocoa solids), chopped
50g walnuts, chopped
80g cocoa powder, sifted
65g plain flour, sifted
1 teaspoon baking powder, sifted
360g caster sugar
4 large eggs

Preheat the oven to 180°C/gas mark 4. Line a 25cm square baking tin with baking parchment.

In a large bowl set over simmering water melt the butter and the chocolate. Mix until smooth. Add the walnuts and stir together.

In a separate bowl mix together the cocoa powder, flour, baking powder and sugar. Add the dry ingredients to the chocolate and nut mixture and stir together well. Beat the eggs and stir into to the chocolate mixture to give a silky consistency.

Pour the brownie mix into the baking tray and cook in the oven for about 25 minutes. Brownies shouldn't be overcooked, so, unlike cakes, you don't want a skewer to come out clean. The brownies should be slightly springy on the outside but still gooey in the middle. Leave to cool in the tray, then carefully transfer to a large board and cut into chunky squares.

LEMON AND RASPBERRY MUFFINS

You can make a lot of different variations of this recipe. At my bakery we use this recipe but vary it to make Orange and Blueberry, Banana and Cinnamon, Apple, Raisin and Raspberry, or Lemon and White Chocolate.

Makes 12

100g unsalted butter, melted

140g light brown sugar

2 eggs

240ml milk

130g plain flour, sifted

2 teaspoon baking powder, sifted

pinch of salt

140g fresh raspberries

1 tablespoon grated lemon zest

Preheat the oven to 180°C/gas mark 4. Line a 12-hole muffin tin with paper cases.

Put the butter in a large mixing bowl with the sugar and whisk together until light and fluffy. Slowly beat in the eggs, a little at a time, followed by the milk. Fold the flour, baking powder and salt into the mixture.

Gently fold the raspberries and lemon zest into the mixture and spoon the batter into the paper cases. Bake in the oven for 20 minutes or until the muffins are lightly golden brown. Check that they are cooked by inserting a skewer into the middle of a muffin; if it comes out clean the muffin is cooked.

Allow to cool for 5 minutes in the tin before transferring to a wire rack to cool.

WHITE CHOCOLATE AND MACADAMIA COOKIES

This is a soft cookie dough which you can wrap in cling film and refrigerate or freeze for whenever you want to use it. Serve with a big glass of cold milk or tuck in your lunchbox for an afternoon treat.

Makes 16

110g butter, softened
170g light brown sugar
60g caster sugar
1 egg
1 teaspoon vanilla extract
260g plain flour
1/2 teaspoon baking soda
1/2 teaspoon baking powder
150g toasted macadamia nuts, chopped
220g white chocolate buttons or chopped chocolate

Preheat the oven to 180°C/gas mark 4. Line two baking trays with baking parchment.

Beat together the butter and sugars until light and fluffy. Beat in the egg, a little at a time, and the vanilla extract.

Sift the flour, baking soda and baking powder into the butter and egg mixture and beat together until the cookie dough comes together. Beat in the nuts and chocolate.

Use your hands to make 16 walnut-sized balls from the dough. Put them on the baking trays and use the back of a spoon to flatten them into discs about 5cm across. Space the cookies about 7.5cm apart because they will expand during cooking.

Bake in the oven for 15-20 minutes or until they are golden brown in colour. Leave to cool on a wire rack.

OCTOBER

Christmas cake

Spiced Butternut
Squash and
Coconut Soup

CHRISTMAS BAKING

The big Christmas Bake was a huge tradition in our house - my granny would bring the recipe for Christmas cake and pudding and Mum would get the ingredients. My sisters, brother and I would weigh and mix ingredients and cut circles of baking parchment. Each of us would make a wish as we stirred the pudding mix and take turns to lick the bowls. We were having fun but we were also learning treasured family recipes, and picking up valuable skills from Granny and Mum. Those days provided a real sense of continuity between the generations in our family.

With my work I spend a good deal of time talking to people about food. Something that keeps coming up with younger people, the pre-prepared food generation, is that they feel disconnected from these traditions. They loved watching their own mums and grans cook but don't have the confidence to do it themselves, simply because they don't cook much at any other time of year. It worries them that they won't have the skills to pass on to their own kids.

So when I started Christmas Baking classes at the cookery school, I wasn't surprised at the uptake or that most of the class were younger than usual. I was delighted when many of them made a pact to do the same again the following October. I know we can't all be with our families but why not get a group of friends together to start an annual tradition of Christmas baking, take pictures, talk about your memories, about how your mother used to bake and keep the tradition alive! Every autumn we keep the grand Christmas baking tradition alive in my bakery and the smells waft throughout the kitchens. Oh yes, Christmas isn't too far away now…

CHRISTMAS CAKE

Traditionally Christmas cakes are made at the end of November, but I always make mine in October to allow more time for the flavours to develop.

Makes 1 cake

450g currants
175g raisins
50g glacé cherries
50g mixed candied peel
4 tablespoons brandy, plus extra for feeding
220g plain flour
$\frac{1}{2}$ teaspoon salt
$\frac{1}{4}$ teaspoon freshly grated nutmeg
$\frac{1}{2}$ teaspoon mixed spice
225g unsalted butter
225g brown sugar
4 large eggs
50g chopped almonds
1 dessertspoon black treacle
grated zest of 1 lemon
grated zest of 1 orange
110g whole blanched almonds (optional)

The day before you want to bake the cake put the dried fruit, cherries and mixed peel in a bowl. Mix the brandy as evenly and thoroughly as possible, then cover the bowl with a clean tea-towel and leave overnight, or for at least 12 hours so that the fruit absorbs the brandy.

Preheat the oven to 130°C/gas mark 1. Grease and line a 20cm round cake tin or an 18cm square tin with baking parchment. Tie a band of brown paper around the outside of the tin for extra protection.

Sift the flour, salt and spices into a large mixing bowl, lifting the sieve high to give the flour a good airing.

In a separate large bowl, using an electric whisk, whisk together the butter and sugar until the mixture is light and fluffy. Beat the eggs in a separate bowl and add them to the creamed mixture a tablespoonful at a time. Keep the whisk running until all the eggs are incorporated; if you add the eggs slowly it is less likely that the mixture will curdle.

Fold the flour and spices into the mixture, using gentle, folding movements so that you keep the air in; do not beat the mixture. Fold in the fruit, peel, chopped almonds, treacle and the grated lemon and orange zests. (The treacle will be easier to measure if you remove the lid and put the tin in a small pan of barely simmering water.)

Use a large kitchen spoon to transfer the mixture into the cake tin, spreading it out evenly with the back of the spoon. If you don't intend to ice the cake lightly drop the whole blanched almonds in circles or squares over the surface.

Cover the top of the cake with a double square of baking
parchment with a 25mm hole in the centre to give extra
protection during the long, slow cooking. Bake the cake on
the lowest shelf of the oven for 4½-4¾ hours. It can
sometimes take up to 30-45 minutes longer than this, but
in any case don't look until at least 4 hours have passed.

Leave the cake to cool in the tin for 30 minutes, then
transfer it to a wire rack to finish cooling. When the cake
is completely cold 'feed' it by making small holes in the
top and base of the cake with a cocktail stick or small
skewer and spoon over a few teaspoons of brandy. Wrap the
cake in a double layer of baking parchment secured with an
elastic band and either wrap it in kitchen foil or store
in an airtight container. If you wish, you can feed it at
intervals until you need to ice or eat it.

MY MUM'S CHRISTMAS PUDDING

Every year my mum makes a Christmas pudding for me and my siblings, as her mother did before her. I love this tradition and plum puddings are a lovely gift.

Makes 2

butter, for greasing
230g plain flour
1 teaspoon mixed spice
1 teaspoon grated nutmeg
50g nibbed almonds
370g soft dark brown sugar
220g shredded suet
220g sultanas
220g currants
220g raisins
170g mixed peel
170g dried white breadcrumbs
6 eggs
5 tablespoons Irish stout
juice of 1 orange
50ml brandy
125ml milk

Butter two 600ml pudding basins.

In a large bowl sift the flour, mixed spice and nutmeg. Mix in the almonds, sugar, suet, dried fruit, mixed peel and breadcrumbs. In a separate bowl combine the eggs, stout, orange juice, brandy and milk. Stir the liquid mixture into the dry ingredients.

Divide the mixture between the pudding basins. For each pudding cut a round of baking parchment 1½ times the size of the rim of the basin. Grease, then fold a single pleat in the paper to allow room for the pudding to expand during cooking. Cover each pudding with parchment and secure with string.

Place each pudding into a saucepan with water halfway up the side. Cover and steam for 6 hours or longer. The longer a pudding cooks, the richer and darker it becomes. Top up each pan with boiling water as required and don't let the water boil dry.

To store: Remove the rounds of baking parchment and replace with new. Wrap each pudding in a cloth and store in a cool dry place until required.

To reheat: Steam each pudding for 2 hours and serve.

Makes 2.8kg

350g seedless raisins
220g sultanas
220g currants
170g mixed peel
350g soft brown sugar
450g cooking apples, peeled, cored
and grated
225g shredded suet
grated rind and juice of 2 oranges
grated rind and juice of 2 lemons
50g nibbed almonds
50g chopped pecan nuts
1 tablespoon mixed spice
1 teaspoon grated nutmeg
150ml brandy

CHRISTMAS MINCEMEAT

I know it sounds strange to roast the mincemeat, but this tip, given to me by my sister Mairead, who is a fabulous cook, really does bring out the flavours.

Mix together all the ingredients, except half the brandy, in a large, ovenproof bowl, cover and leave to stand overnight.

Preheat the oven to 110°C/gas mark ¼.

Cover the bowl with kitchen foil and cook in the oven for about 3 hours. Allow to cool, then mix in the rest of the brandy and transfer to sterilised jars (see page 204).

HALLOWEEN

Halloween is absolutely the time to embrace your inner child or perhaps your inner goth. Just think graveyards, ghosts, ghouls, creepy crawlies, body parts and lashings of blood. Get yourself an icing gun, three or four different food colours (red is essential), a paint brush and a sheet of roll out royal icing. Any flat biscuit serves as the body of a creepy crawly or a ghoul, just paint or ice on gruesome features. Hovis biscuits make great tombstones. Use your icing gun to apply guest's names.

Liquorice sticks are good for spider legs, they are bendy but hold their shape when attached to biscuits, cakes or other sweets. Just add a couple of liquorish allsorts eyes.
Gob stoppers make great eyeballs and Snowballs or little Ferrero Rocher are great for attaching ears and tails to. Slightly under set jelly is perfect for green slime.

For the adults, what about a blood red wine punch? Just drop a dry ice pellet in for that eerie, fog effect. Devils on horseback are always a winner. Go on you devil, tease out some candy floss cobwebs and dribble some red food colouring from the corner of your mouth. Cue villainous laugh, 'Mee, haw, haw, haw'.

BLOODTHIRSTY SQUASH

Delight children and adults alike with this ghoulish drink for a spooky occasion. Looks great served as a punch at a party too.

Serves 10

1 litre lemonade
1 litre cranberry juice
juice of 3-4 limes

Fill a clean washing-up glove with water, secure the end with a freezer clip or rubber band and place it in the freezer overnight.

Stir together the lemonade, cranberry juice and lime juice and pour into a punch bowl or large jug.

Remove the hand from the freezer and use scissors to remove the glove. Put the frozen hand in the punch bowl and serve.

5 large egg whites, at
room temperature
115g caster sugar
115g icing sugar
dark chocolate chips, to
decorate

GHOST MERINGUES

These are so much fun to make with children. Easy peasy too, I promise you. I used to make them with the kids that came for my Halloween cookery class.

Preheat the oven to 110°C/gas mark ¼. Line two baking trays with non-stick liner or baking parchment (meringue can stick on greaseproof paper and kitchen foil).

Tip the egg whites into a large, clean mixing bowl (not plastic). Beat them on medium speed with an electric hand whisk until the mixture resembles a fluffy cloud and stands up in stiff peaks when the blades are lifted.

Increase the speed of the whisk and start to add the caster sugar, a dessertspoon at a time. Continue beating for 3-4 seconds between each addition. It's important to add the sugar slowly to prevent the meringue from oozing later, but don't over-beat. When it is ready the mixture should be thick and glossy.

Sift one-third of the icing sugar over the mixture, then gently fold it in with a big metal spoon or rubber spatula. Continue to sift and fold in the icing sugar, a third at a time. Don't overmix. The mixture should now look smooth and billowy, almost like a snow drift.

Scoop the mixture into a piping bag with a 1.5-2cm nozzle. Squeeze into ghost-like shapes about 3cm apart. Carefully add the chocolate chip 'eyes'. Bake in the oven for 1½ hours so that the meringues are still white but can be lifted from the parchment without sticking. Turn off the oven, leave the door ajar and leave the meringues until cold. The meringues will now keep in an airtight tin for up to 2 weeks or frozen for a month.

SPICED PUMPKIN CAKE

The cake is quite light but the frosting is sinful! Make the base the day before, and then make up the icing the day you are going to eat it.

Makes 1 cake

160g unsalted butter, softened
160g dark brown sugar
160g sugar
4 eggs
300g pumpkin purée
120ml buttermilk
1 teaspoon vanilla extract
300g flour
2 teaspoons baking powder
1 teaspoon baking soda
1 teaspoon ground cinnamon
½ teaspoon ground nutmeg

For the Icing:

130g cream cheese
40g unsalted butter, softened
70g pumpkin purée
1 teaspoon vanilla extract
1 tablespoon freshly squeezed
orange juice
1 teaspoon grated orange zest
400g icing sugar

Preheat the oven to 180°C/gas mark 4. Grease the bases and sides of two 25cm cake tins and line the bases with baking parchment.

Put the butter and sugars in a large mixing bowl and use an electric whisk to cream them together until light and fluffy. Whisk in the eggs, one at a time, then add the pumpkin purée, buttermilk and vanilla extract. Combine well.

Sift in the flour, baking powder, baking soda, cinnamon and nutmeg and combine until smooth. Pour the mixture into the cake tins and tap the sides to release any air bubbles. Bake in the oven for 35-40 minutes or until the sponge is lightly golden brown. Check by inserting a skewer into the centre of the cake; if it comes out clean the cake is cooked. Allow the cakes to cool in the tins and then move to a wire rack.

Meanwhile, make the icing. Beat together the cream cheese, butter, pumpkin purée, vanilla extract, orange juice and zest with an electric whisk until smooth. Add the icing sugar and continue to beat until light and fluffy.

Top one of the cakes with half the icing and put the other cake on top. Cover the top of the cake with the remaining icing.

MARSHMALLOW BRAINS

You can make these the day before you throw a Halloween party as they keep well. Also try adding candy-coated chocolate drops or chocolate chips to the mix.

Makes 10

85g popping corn
1 tablespoon vegetable oil, plus extra for shaping
25g butter
85g marshmallows

Line a baking tray with baking parchment.

Put the popping corn and oil in a large pan set over a medium heat. Stir the kernels around the pan to coat in the oil.

When the kernels start to pop, place a lid firmly on top and turn down the heat to low. Cook for about 5 minutes, shaking the pan often to stop the popcorn burning or sticking, until the corn has stopped popping. Tip into a bowl, discarding any unopened kernels.

Heat the butter and marshmallows over a low heat until melted. Pour the mixture over the popcorn and mix well until coated. Lightly rub oil over your hands and shape the popcorn into small balls. Put on the baking tray and leave to set.

FREAKY FINGERS

Glacé cherries work the best for this recipe but you could also use chocolate chips for black fingernails.

Makes 20

100g caster sugar
100g butter
1 egg yolk
200g plain flour
½ teaspoon vanilla extract
a pinch of salt
glacé cherries, cut into fingernail shapes or strawberry jam

Preheat the oven to 180°C/gas mark 4. Line a baking tray with baking parchment.

Put all the ingredients, except the glacé cherries or jam, in a food-processor and whizz just until a ball of dough forms.

Tear off pieces of dough about the size of a golf ball and use your hands to roll them into finger-size cylinders; you should get about 20 in total.

Place the fingers on the baking tray, spacing them a little apart because they will spread during baking, and use a knife to make a few cuts, close together, to represent knuckles.

Position a nail-shaped cherry at one tip of each finger or use strawberry jam and bake in the oven for 10-12 minutes just until firm. Leave to cool.

NUTTY TOFFEE APPLES

You can't have a Halloween party without toffee apples. You can omit the nuts if you if wish, but definitely not the toffee!

Makes 6 apples

6 small wooden ice lolly sticks

6 eating apples

220g sugar

110ml water

30g butter

2 tablespoons golden syrup

4 tablespoons finely chopped mixed nuts

Line a baking tray with non-stick baking parchment. Push the wooden sticks halfway into the apples at the stalk end.

Dissolve the sugar and water in a thick-bottomed pan over a gentle heat. Add the butter and syrup to the mixture and bring to the boil. Continue to boil, without stirring, until the toffee reaches 290°C (use a sugar thermometer to measure this).

Remove the pan from the heat and gently stir in the nuts.

Carefully dip each apple into the toffee, making sure that each one is well coated, and set aside to harden on the baking tray.

BAKED CINNAMON AND GOLDEN RAISIN APPLES

My dad used to make these for us when we were growing up. I love them so much, not only because of the memory of him making them but also because they are what October means to me...

Serves 4

4 cooking apples
100g brown sugar
2 teaspoons honey
2 teaspoons ground cinnamon
50g golden raisins
16 cloves
20g butter

Preheat the oven to 180°C/gas mark 4.

Remove the apple cores with a corer and use a teaspoon to enlarge the cavity to double the size. Stand the apples in an ovenproof dish.

In a small bowl mix together the sugar, honey, cinnamon and raisins and fill each apple with the mixture. Pierce each apple with 4 cloves, add a small piece of butter to the top of each apple and cook in the oven for 20 minutes.

Serve hot with whipped cream.

SPICED BUTTERNUT SQUASH AND COCONUT SOUP

This combination works so well together. If you are not a fan of coconut milk then just replace with vegetable or chicken stock and try adding a little chorizo.

Serves 4

20g butter

1kg butternut squash, skinned, deseeded and cut into 2.5cm pieces

1 teaspoon ground cumin

1 teaspoon garam masala

2 garlic cloves, crushed

200g onions, chopped

700ml hot vegetable stock

300ml coconut milk

sea salt and freshly ground black pepper

Melt the butter in a heavy-bottomed saucepan, add the squash, spices, garlic and onions and season with salt and pepper. Cover and leave to simmer, stirring occasionally, for about 15 minutes.

Stir in the stock and coconut milk and bring the soup to the boil. When the squash is tender the soup is ready to be blended using a food-processor or hand blender. Serve hot.

BUTTERNUT SQUASH AND PARMESAN RISOTTO

You need to be patient when making a risotto, adding a little stock at a time, stirring and tasting as you go, but it's so worth the time and effort.

Serves 4

70g butter, plus extra for finishing
1 shallot, finely chopped
2 garlic cloves, crushed
300g risotto rice
100ml dry white wine
1kg butternut squash
700ml hot vegetable stock
150g grated Parmesan cheese, plus extra for serving
50g mascarpone cheese
sea salt and freshly ground black pepper

Melt the butter in a large saucepan, add the shallots and garlic and cook gently for 3-4 minutes, until softened. Add the rice and stir for a minute to coat the rice in the butter. Pour in the white wine and let it bubble for a few minutes to allow the alcohol to evaporate.

Meanwhile, prepare the butternut squash. Peel the squash, take out all the seeds and chop the flesh into small cubes. Add the butternut squash to the risotto rice, and stir well.

Every couple of minutes add a ladle of stock to the pan. Stir and allow the rice to absorb the juices. Repeat until all the stock has been absorbed.

When the rice is tender, stir in the Parmesan and mascarpone cheese and season to taste with salt and pepper. Scatter over extra Parmesan before serving.

WILD MUSHROOMS WRAPPED IN PAPPARDELLE AND PANCETTA

This is a alightly more delicate version of the traditional carbonara. If you can't get fresh wild mushrooms then use good-quality dried ones and rehydrate them. You could add a few button mushrooms into the mix, too. Halved and roasted cherry tomatoes and a few torn fresh basil leaves also work well.

Serves 4

60g butter
120g pancetta, chopped
1 garlic clove, crushed
200g wild mushrooms
juice of 1/2 lemon
200ml crème fraîche
70g Parmesan cheese, plus extra for serving
1 teaspoon finely chopped sage
450g pappardelle, cooked al dente
sea salt and freshly ground black pepper

Set a saucepan over a medium heat and melt the butter. Add the pancetta and cook for 3 minutes. Stir in the garlic, then the mushrooms and cook for a further 2 minutes.

Add the lemon juice, crème fraîche, Parmesan and sage to the pan and stir well. Cook for 5 minutes or until the sauce has thickened a little.

Stir in the cooked pasta and combine well. Season to taste with salt and pepper. Serve with plenty of grated Parmesan cheese.

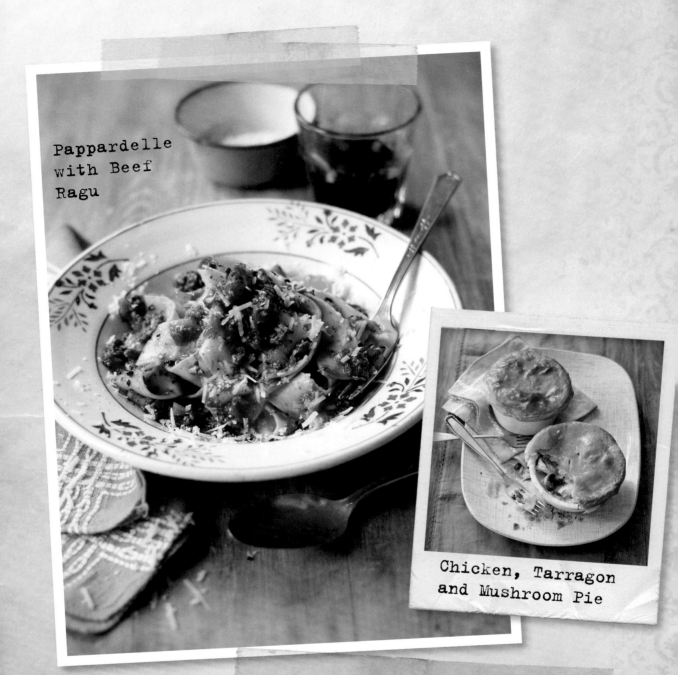

Pappardelle
with Beef
Ragu

Chicken, Tarragon
and Mushroom Pie

NOVEMBER

MOVIE NIGHTS

What is it with popcorn and crunchy snacks in cinemas?
It's like encouraging teenagers to play *Grand Theft Auto*
in church. Years ago I organized picnic baskets, filled
with artisan produce, for cinema-goers at the Cork Film
Festival. It was so civilised, romantic and quiet! It was
for an event at the Kino cinema, Ireland's only
independent art house cinema, now sadly closed. It made
me aware of how closely film and food are linked.

Have you noticed how films about food always involve
passion and sensuality? Think of the denial and self-
gratification in the lavish banquet in *Babette's Feast*; of
how the sweetness of the confectionary in *Chocolat* melts
the sourness of the bourgeoisie; and how Tilda Swinton is
seduced by the sublime food of the chef in *I am Love*.

I've given up on multiplex cinemas. It's such a soulless
experience. Nowadays I occasionally go to art house or
independent cinemas, the Irish Film Institute in Dublin
is great. But on a cold November evening I am happier to
watch movies at home and cook. I think film and food are
very natural pleasures to mix. I like to match the food
I am making to the world of the film I am watching. Just
try it! Curl up with *Cinema Paradiso* and a bowl of
Pappardalle; tuck into a spicy curry and watch *Slumdog
Millionaire*. Or for the ultimate in romance watch
Casablanca with couscous and a lamb tagine. This could
be the beginning of a beautiful friendship!

SMOKED HADDOCK AND MUSSEL CHOWDER

When I took this off the menu at my restaurant, there was such an outcry from customers that we had to put it back on after just 2 weeks. I'm not sure I can give it a better introduction than that! Make sure you buy undyed smoked haddock.

Serves 4

20g butter
1 onion, finely diced
1 leek, finely sliced
2 garlic cloves, crushed
100ml dry white wine
300ml fish stock
200ml milk
200g potatoes, peeled and diced
600g undyed smoked haddock, skin removed and cut into small chunks
16 fresh mussels, scrubbed and debearded
150ml single cream
6 chives, finely sliced
sea salt and freshly ground black pepper

Set a saucepan over a medium heat and melt the butter. Stir in the onion, leek and garlic. Reduce the heat, cover and leave to sweat for 5 minutes.

Remove the pan from the heat and add the wine. Return the pan to the heat and cook for a further 3-4 minutes. Pour in the stock, milk and potatoes and bring to the boil. Reduce the heat and simmer for 10 minutes.

Stir in the haddock and mussels and continue to cook for 5 minutes. Add the cream, chives and season to taste with salt and pepper. Cook for a further 5 minutes.

PARMESAN AND ROSEMARY POLENTA CHIPS

A favourite of mine after a trip to Emilio Romania in Italy. A great snack for movie watching, a great side dish with roast chicken, and great for party food.

Serves 8

500ml water
1kg polenta
200g Parmesan cheese, grated
vegetable oil, for deep-frying
a few sprigs of rosemary
sea salt and freshly ground black pepper

Line a baking tray with greaseproof paper.

Bring the water to the boil in a large saucepan, add the polenta and stir over medium-high heat for about 20 minutes.

Reduce the heat, stir in the Parmesan, season to taste with salt and pepper and continue to stir for a further 5 minutes.

Spread the polenta in the baking tray to an even depth of about 1.5cm. Allow to cool and then cut the polenta into chip-like shapes.

Deep-fry the chips and toss them in sea salt and finely chopped rosemary to serve.

SPICY CHICKEN WINGS

I love serving these spicy and sweet wings with a cooling blue cheese dip. Just whisk together 100g blue cheese, 140ml sour cream and the juice of $\frac{1}{2}$ lemon.

Makes 36

36 chicken wings
6 garlic cloves, crushed
1 teaspoon freshly grated ginger
2 teaspoons sesame oil
60ml light soy sauce
2 tablespoons rice wine vinegar
2 tablespoons vegetable oil
2 tablespoons Tabasco sauce
1 tablespoon brown sugar
sea salt and freshly ground black pepper

To serve

6 chives, snipped
240ml soured cream

Preheat the oven to 180°C/gas mark 4. Line a baking tray with kitchen foil.

Season the wings with salt and pepper, put them on the baking tray and bake in the oven for 45 minutes.

Make a vinaigrette by whisking together the remaining ingredients. Pour the vinaigrette over the wings while they are hot and toss them around so that the wings soak up all the dressing.

Scatter the chives over the wings and serve with soured cream.

MINI SPICY MEATBALLS

To make these more moist add 100g ricotta cheese.
Delicious served with my Tomato, Basil and Olive Sauce
on page 195

Makes 40

3kg minced beef
6 tablespoons chopped
fresh coriander
4 red chillies, finely
chopped
6 garlic cloves, crushed
2 onions, finely chopped
3 eggs, lightly beaten
flour, for dusting
olive oil, for frying
sea salt and freshly
ground black pepper

Preheat the oven to 180°C/gas mark 4.

In a large bowl mix together the beef,
coriander, chillies, garlic, onions and eggs.
Season to taste with salt and pepper.

Roll a teaspoon of the beef mixture into a
ball, dust it in flour and put to one side.
Repeat with the rest of the mixture.

Set a frying pan over a medium heat and add
some olive oil. Gently sauté the meatballs and
then cook them in the oven for 15 minutes.

Serve with Roasted Tomato, Basil and Olive
Sauce (see page 195) to dip the meatballs in.

CHICKEN, BROCCOLI AND PARMESAN BAKE

A crispy topping, creamy base, with crunchy broccoli bites – delicious. Serve with a big green salad.

Serves 4

2 tablespoons olive oil

2 skinless fillets of chicken, diced

1 onion, finely chopped

2 garlic cloves, crushed

30g butter

30g flour

200ml milk

100g Parmesan cheese, grated

10 basil leaves, torn

400g broccoli, quartered and blanched

100g breadcrumbs

50g pine nuts, chopped

sea salt and freshly ground black pepper

Preheat the oven to 180°C/gas mark 4.

Set a saucepan over a medium heat and add the oil. Stir in the chicken, season with salt and pepper and cook for 3 minutes, searing on all sides. Stir in the onion and garlic and cook for a further 2 minutes.

Set a separate saucepan over a low heat to make the sauce. Melt the butter, stir in the flour and continue to stir until the flour is cooked and you get a paste (roux). Whisk in the milk, a little at a time, until you have a thick, creamy béchamel sauce. Whisk in the Parmesan and basil and season with salt and pepper.

Tip the seared chicken and onions into a roasting tin or large ovenproof dish and arrange the broccoli around the chicken. Pour the Parmesan and basil sauce over the chicken. Sprinkle the breadcrumbs and pine nuts on top and cook in the oven for 20 minutes.

CHICKEN, TARRAGON AND MUSHROOM PIE

This is comfort food at its best. I made mini versions
of this recipe for the designer Anya Hindmarch's launch
in Ireland, they were delicious. They freeze perfectly
too.

Serves 4

30g butter

4 skinless chicken
fillets, diced

1 leek, finely sliced

280g button mushrooms,
quartered

1 tablespoon flour

250ml milk

100ml single cream

2 tablespoons chopped
tarragon leaves

500g pack of puff pastry
(use butter puff or
brush ordinary puff with
a little butter)

1 egg, beaten

Preheat the oven to 200°C/gas mark 6.

Set a large pan over a medium heat and melt the
butter. Add the chicken, season with salt and pepper
and cook for 5 minutes. Stir in the leek and cook for
a further minute.

Add the mushrooms to the pan and cook for 3 minutes.
Sprinkle over the flour, stir and cook for another
minute, then pour in the milk and cream and allow to
cook until the sauce has thickened. Stir in the
chopped tarragon.

Roll out the pastry and cut it into four pieces big
enough to cover four small pie dishes. Spoon the
chicken mixture into the dishes and brush the rims
with beaten egg.

Lift the pastry on to the pies, trimming off any
excess. Press down and crimp the edges with a fork.
Cut a couple of slits in the pastry to let the steam
out and brush all over with the rest of the egg. Bake
in the oven for 15-20 minutes or until the pastry is
crisp and golden brown.

LEMON AND ROSEMARY ROAST CHICKEN

I do a roast chicken about once a month, investing in good-quality, organic chicken because it tastes far better.

Serves 4

100g butter
2 lemons
4 sprigs of rosemary, finely chopped
5 garlic cloves, crushed
1 whole chicken
900g potatoes, peeled and quartered
16 shallots, left whole
sea salt and freshly ground black pepper
olive oil

Preheat the oven to 180°C/gas mark 4.

In a bowl mix the together the butter, lemon juice and zest, the finely chopped rosemary leaves and garlic and season with salt and pepper. Spread half the flavoured butter over the chicken.

Chop up the lemon skins and place them in the cavity of the chicken along with the rosemary stalks left once you have removed the leaves.

Set a roasting tin over a low heat and add the remaining flavoured butter. Melt the butter, increase the heat and toss the potatoes and shallots until well coated. Arrange the vegetables around the sides of the roasting tin and put the chicken in the centre.

Roast in the oven for 1½ hours. Every 20 minutes spoon the juices in the roasting tin over the chicken to enhance the flavour.

CHILLI

This is always better the next day as the flavours
develop overnight. This chilli, some sour cream,
guacamole and rice in front of an open fire and a great
movie is November heaven to me.

Serves 4

1 tablespoon olive oil
1 onion, finely chopped
3 garlic cloves, crushed
1 red pepper, cored,
deseeded and finely
chopped
1 tablespoon freshly
grated ginger
1 teaspoon hot chilli
powder
1 teaspoon paprika
1 teaspoon ground
cinnamon
1 teaspoon ground cumin
500g minced beef
400g can chopped
tomatoes
1 teaspoon dried oregano
1 teaspoon brown sugar
2 tablespoons tomato
purée
300ml hot stock
(preferably beef stock)
410g can red kidney
beans, rinsed and
drained
sea salt and freshly
ground black pepper

Place a large saucepan or casserole dish over a medium
heat and add the oil. Stir in the onion, garlic, red
pepper, ginger, chilli powder, paprika, cinnamon and
cumin, cover and leave to simmer for 2-3 minutes.

In a separate pan brown the minced beef, season with
salt and pepper and add to the onion mixture.

Stir in the tomatoes, dried oregano, sugar, tomato
purée and stock. Bring to the boil, reduce the heat
and allow to simmer for 20 minutes. Lastly stir in the
kidney beans and cook for a further 5 minutes.

Burrito - To make a
burrito spoon
some chilli into
a tortilla with
shredded lettuce
and some Lime and
Tomato Guacamole
(see page 140)
and wrap it up.

PAPPARDELLE WITH BEEF RAGU

The secret to a great ragu is, the longer you leave it to simmer over a low heat, the better it tastes. If it gets too dry just stir in some water. If you can't get pappardelle then use spaghetti. This freezes well, so double up and save for a rainy, hungry evening.

Serves 4

2-3 tablespoons olive oil

25g butter

1 onion, finely diced

1 carrot, finely diced

1/2 celery stick, finely diced

4 garlic cloves, crushed

1kg minced beef

400ml red wine

600g can chopped tomatoes

2 tablespoons tomato purée

2 teaspoons dried oregano

1 teaspoon freshly grated nutmeg

600g fresh pappardelle

100g Parmesan cheese, grated

sea salt and freshly ground black pepper

Set a casserole over a medium heat and add the oil and butter. Add the onion, carrot, celery and garlic, stir and cook for 5 minutes or until softened.

Stir in the beef and season with salt and pepper. Cook, stirring occasionally, until the beef has turned a light brown colour. Pour in the wine and leave to simmer for about 20 minutes.

Stir in the tomatoes, tomato purée, dried oregano and nutmeg, season with salt and pepper and mix well. Reduce the heat and leave to simmer for an hour or more if you can. The longer you allow it to simmer the more tender and flavoursome the ragu becomes. Add a little beef stock if it becomes too thick.

Put a large saucepan of salted water over a high heat and bring to the boil. Tip in the pappardelle and continue to stir for 2 minutes. Cook until al dente and drain, reserving 2 tablespoons cooking water. Return the pasta to the saucepan (off the heat) and stir in the cooking water followed by the ragu.

Serve with grated Parmesan sprinkled over.

NAAN BREAD

I have a wonderful Indian chef working for me called Jamille. He taught me how to make Naan bread and now we serve them with our house Indian Chicken Curry. You can add a whole variety of toppings, see below.

Makes 5

For the dough

250g plain flour
2 teaspoons sugar
½ teaspoon salt
½ teaspoon baking
powder
110–130ml milk
2 tablespoons vegetable
oil, plus extra for
greasing

For the topping

nigella seeds, poppy
seeds or sesame seeds,
or chopped garlic and
fresh coriander
melted butter

Make the dough. Sift the flour, sugar, salt and baking powder into a bowl. In another bowl mix together the milk and oil.

Make a well in the centre of the flour mixture and pour in the liquid. Slowly mix the dough, working from the centre and incorporating the flour from the edges of the well, to make a smooth, soft dough. Knead well for 8-10 minutes, adding a little flour if the dough is too sticky.

Place the dough into an oiled bowl, cover with a damp tea-towel and leave in a warm place for 10-15 minutes. Form the dough into five balls.

Preheat the grill to medium and put a heavy baking tray on the upper shelf of the grill to heat.

Roll the dough balls out quite thinly, ideally in a teardrop shape. Sprinkle over your chosen topping and press into the surface of the dough. Place the naan bread on the hot baking tray and grill for 1-2 minutes or until lightly browned. Brush with butter and serve hot.

INDIAN CURRY

I absolutely love this recipe. You could try replacing the chicken with lamb if you wish. Serve with raita.

Serves 4

7.5cm piece of fresh ginger, peeled and finely chopped

6 garlic cloves, chopped

1 onion, finely chopped

1 tablespoon ground coriander

1 tablespoon ground cumin

1/2 teaspoon ground turmeric

1 teaspoon cayenne pepper

200ml water

3 tablespoons vegetable oil

4 skinless chicken fillets, diced

200ml coconut milk

100g can chopped tomatoes

300g butternut squash, diced

24 French beans

2 tablespoons fresh coriander, chopped

sea salt and freshly ground black pepper

Put the ginger, garlic, onion and spices into an food-processor with 100ml water and blend to a fine paste. You may have to push the mixture down with a spatula from time to time. Set aside.

Heat the oil in a large, wide, preferably non-stick pan, over a high heat. Stir in the chicken, season with salt and pepper and cook for 3-4 minutes.

Add the spicy paste to the pan with the remaining water, coconut milk and tomatoes. Bring to the boil, stir in the butternut squash, cover, reduce the heat to low and cook for 20 minutes.

Stir in the French beans and cook for a further 5 minutes. Remove the pan from the heat and stir in the fresh coriander. Check the seasoning and serve with naan bread and raita.

RAITA

Serves 4

1/2 cucumber

1/2 red onion, finely chopped

500ml Greek yogurt

2 tablespoons chopped mint leaves

2 tablespoons chopped fresh coriander leaves

sea salt and freshly ground black pepper

Coarsely grate the cucumber into a bowl and squeeze it with your hands to remove as much juice as possible.

In a bowl mix together the cucumber, onion, yogurt, mint and coriander. Season with salt and pepper. Cover with clingfilm and chill until you are ready to serve.

APPLE, CINNAMON AND RAISIN BREAD AND BUTTER PUDDING

I'm a huge fan of bread and butter pudding. You can omit the apple if you wish, and add melted chocolate. Or sometimes, if I have leftover brioche I'll use it for a super decadent bread and butter pudding.

Serves 5

400ml milk

400ml single cream

100g caster sugar

6 eggs

1 teaspoon vanilla extract

1 tablespoon ground cinnamon

16 slices of white bread, cut into triangles

200g cooking apples, quartered, cored and sliced

100g golden raisins

Preheat the oven to 160°C/gas mark 3.

Set a saucepan over a medium heat, add the milk, cream and sugar and mix well together. Cook until the sugar has dissolved, then set aside to cool.

Whisk the eggs in a large bowl and stir in the vanilla extract and cinnamon. Whisk in the milk mixture.

Overlap the bread pieces and apple slices in an ovenproof dish and pour over the egg mixture. Use your hands to push the bread gently into the egg mixture so that it is completed immersed. Scatter the raisins over the top of the pudding. Bake in the oven for 45 minutes.

HOMEMADE CHRISTMAS WREATH

I've been a huge fan of Ruth Monahan's creativity for a long time. Imagine a modern day Audrey Hepburn in the most glorious flower shop and you have a picture of Ruth. Since establishing Appassionata Flowers (www.appassionata.ie) in 2004 with her husband Ultan, Ruth has brought a fresh and inspirational approach to flowers in Dublin. She started in her kitchen but has grown Appassionata into one of the market leaders in the field of quality floristry design. I'm so happy that she is part of my book, and here is her guide to making a beautiful Christmas wreath.

Preparation

Making the Christmas wreath is one of the nicest things to do in preparation for the festive season. The best time to start planning your wreath is in late November, so you will be ready to display it from about 2 weeks before the big day. It looks amazing to see all the doorways dressed with wreaths individually created to suit the person living there.

Before starting your wreath you need to consider several things. Your front door will define your wreath's look and feel. The colour and size of your door will act as a background for your festive display. Also, consider what you will hang the wreath on so that it is secure and will defy rain, wind and snow, not to mention children's curious hands.

Decide your preferred colourway. Do you want to go red and traditional, dusky blue and vintage, or shun the traditional festive colours and make it pink? It's always good to have saved some autumnal hydrangea in your preferred colour scheme, and we always have old heads hanging in bunches around the studio and shop ready to dress our Christmas wreaths.

Your tools are the secret to a beautiful and successful wreath. You will need a glue gun, a wire frame base or a noble pine base, a reel of wire, lots of noble pine and a gorgeous ribbon to adorn the doorway. How you dress your wreath comes down to you prefered textures and scents. You might like to try eucalyptus and lavender (for a calming scent as you reach home), skimmia (can be bought as plant or cut), thistle (in blue or white), berries (such as hypericum, viburnum and ilex), or dried hydrangea (it looks fresh as the day it was cut and beats silk versions hands down). Noble pine can be bought in bunches from a florist or garden centre, and other elements you could grab from the garden or a garden centre include rosemary, moss or lichen, cones, cinnamon and mini apples.

Making a Wreath

I usually lay old newspapers out on my kitchen table, place all of the various elements in groups ready for action and have the glue gun heating up.

First cut the noble pine for the base of your wreath. Start the reel wire by winding it onto the frame. Gradually place the pine in layers

The best way to work is to go layer by layer each time using the glue gun to secure the element, e.g. eucalyptus, followed by skimmia, berries and thistle. Make sure each is sitting securely in the pine base. Add lavender, rosemary and extra berries to fill in any gaps. The wreath should look balanced and similar from all angles.

If using cinnamon and cones, wire them first. We usually cut a long cinnamon stick into three and fasten with a knot of ribbon. Reel wire wrapped around the stack of three with a long piece left to act as a stalk works well for placing into the wreath. Leave a gap where you would like to place the ribbon, wrap reel wire around the wreath and leave a long double strand trailing. Tie ribbon in a gorgeous four loop bow with trailing elements. Give your wreath a good spray of water before hanging so that it glistens, attach to the door securely with the wire and be the envy of all your neighbours!

along the circular frame. Continue binding the wire around and around the pine and frame until you have created a substantial base. You want the wreath to look bushy and full.

Now cut more pine in shorter pieces and continue the binding process. Keep turning the wreath after each insertion as this will help to create a nice full look. Trim any unruly pieces. Keep the wreath diameter to approximately 40cm as this is the best dimension for a regular front door.

Separate the hydrangea heads into smaller pieces (unless you want the hydrangea to be completely dominant). Using the glue gun, add glue to the base of the stalk and insert at right angles into the pine. Work clockwise and keep turning the wreath to ensure evenness of placement.

All other elements should be cut short at an angle for easier insertion.

> **TIP** Keep it sprayed with water every few days to keep it looking like the day it was made, otherwise the leaves will go curly and the berries all crinkly.

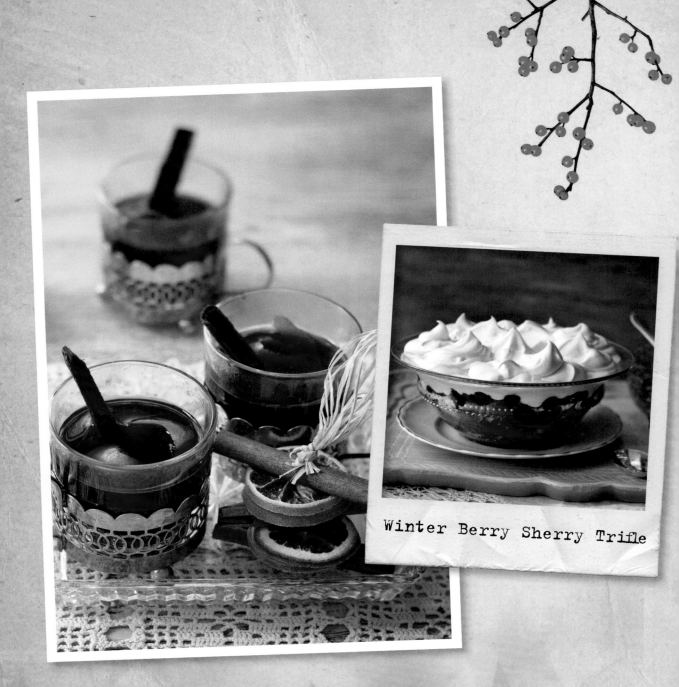

Winter Berry Sherry Trifle

DECEMBER

CHRISTMAS TRADITIONS

I love the way Christmas both passes on traditions and creates new ones. The first Christmas I had in my own home in Monkstown, Dublin, changed the whole way I thought about Christmas. It unleashed my inner Christmas fairy. I decorated the tree with old hand-me-down decorations and tied little birds, cherries and figs to the branches. I tied cinnamon sticks and dried orange skin into little bundles and threw them on the open fire to give the house a wonderful spicy smell. After Mass on Christmas day it was home for a hearty brunch. To work up an appetite for Christmas lunch, which was served at five o'clock, we had a huge walk in the afternoon. Making the centrepieces and an afternoon walk have become set in stone household traditions.

A Christmas tradition I have established for myself is a shopping spree in London a month or so before Christmas. I always visit Fortnum and Mason on Piccadilly - the smell as soon as you walk in is essence of Christmas bottled. It's not just the wonderful foods I love, but the beautiful tins and packaging too. I will always drop into the luxury stationers, Smythson, for gifts. They do really funky coloured notebooks with little messages embossed on the front, like the "make it happen" notebook. One unapologetically indulgent visit I make is to the Fumoir, the art deco bar in Claridge's. I'd go just to look at the beautiful cocktail glasses, never mind the intoxicating drinks! And finally, something I have done since my twenties, I go to the opera at Covent Garden and have a meal at the fish restaurant, J.Sheekey. I end my visit with a walk to Trafalgar Square to see the Christmas tree that Norway traditionally sends Britain every year.

POMEGRANATE CHAMPAGNE

This is a fun cocktail, the colour is just so Christmassy. A good prosecco like Valdo would work perfectly here. Buy a couple of fresh pomegranates and pop a few of the seeds into the glasses.

Makes 8

crushed ice
500ml pomegranate juice
100ml ginger ale
70ml brandy
1 bottle Champagne or
sparkling wine

Fill a large jug two-thirds of the way with crushed ice. Add the rest of the ingredients and mix well.

BAKED VACHERIN

Gooey, easy and yummy. You can use other semi-soft cheeses too, such as Gubbeen or Durrus Irish Farmhouse. Add a little bit of crushed garlic or finely chopped fresh thyme.

Serves 4

500g box vacherin cheese
50ml dry white wine

Preheat the oven to 180°C/gas mark 4. Wrap the base of the box containing the cheese in kitchen foil.

Cut a cross on the top of the cheese and pour over the wine. Put it on a baking tray and cook in the oven for 15-20 minutes, depending on how ripe the cheese is.

Serve the cheese in the box, and let your guests scoop out the gooey cheese with warm crusty bread.

PARMESAN CHEESE STRAWS

These are such fun to make. You can use any hard cheese that you wish and dip them in sesame seeds if you fancy the idea. Perfect for serving on their own or with dips.

Makes 26

1 egg
1 tablespoon water
500g sheet of ready-rolled puff pastry
100g Parmesan cheese, grated
1 teaspoon dried oregano leaves (optional)

Preheat the oven to 180°C/gas mark 4. Grease a baking tray.

In a small bowl whisk together the egg and water and set aside.

Unfold the pastry on a lightly floured surface roll it out to a 35 × 25cm rectangle. Cut it in half lengthways and brush both halves with the egg and water mixture.

Sprinkle the cheese and oregano, if using, over one rectangle and place the other rectangle on top, egg side down. Roll gently with a rolling pin to seal. Cut the pastry crossways into 26 strips, each about 1cm wide.

Twist the strips and place them 5cm apart on the baking tray, pressing down the ends. Brush with the egg and water mixture and bake in the oven for 10 minutes or until golden.

SESAME AND FENNEL MINI SAUSAGE ROLLS

These freeze extremely well and are delicious served with piccalilli or my House Chutney (see page 212).

Makes 20

400g sausagemeat or sausages

2 tablespoons chopped flatleaf parsley

375g sheet of ready-rolled puff pastry

1 beaten egg, to glaze

1 tablespoon fennel seeds

1 tablespoon sesame seeds

sea salt and freshly ground black pepper

Preheat the oven to 180°C/gas mark 4.

Put the sausagemeat and flatleaf parsley in mixing bowl, season with salt and pepper and stir well. Set aside.

Unroll the pastry on to a lightly floured board and cut it in half lengthways to give two rectangles, each about 25cm long.

Halve the sausage mixture and roll each half into a cylinder, about 25cm long. Spread each roll along the length of each pastry strip, leaving a 1cm edge. Tightly roll the pastry around the sausagemeat and brush the ends with the beaten egg to secure. Use a sharp knife to cut each roll into 10 pieces, each about 2.5cm long, and place them on a baking tray.

Brush more egg over the pastry and sprinkle the fennel and sesame seeds on top of the sausage rolls. Cook in the oven for 25-35 minutes until the pastry is puffed and crisp and the meat has cooked through.

CRAB AND AVOCADO TOASTS

This is a staple of mine to serve at Christmas parties. They are the perfect bite, and look so pretty. You can also use this recipe as a salad for a starter or lunch. Just bed the plates with lots of fresh rocket, then sprinkle the crab mix over, and instead of mashing the avocado, slice it and arrange on top of the crab mix. Serve the toasted baguettes on the side.

Serves 6

1 French baguette

2 tablespoons extra virgin olive oil.

200g crab meat, cooked

2 teaspoons lime juice

1 tablespoon chopped mint

2 Hass avocados

a pinch of cayenne pepper

sea salt and freshly ground black pepper

Preheat the oven to 180°C/gas mark 4.

Thinly slice the baguette and lightly brush the slices with oil. Transfer to a baking tray and cook in the oven for 3-4 minutes or until lightly golden.

In a bowl mix together the crab meat and mint and season with salt and pepper. In a separate, smaller bowl mash the avocado flesh with lime juice, a pinch each of salt and cayenne pepper.

Spread the mashed avocado over the sliced bread, top with the crab mixture and serve.

ORANGE AND CINNAMON MINCE PIE ROULADES

I came up with this recipe at the cookery school when I was looking for stress-free foods I could serve over Christmas. They are so delicious, best served warm and with double cream.

Makes 12

50g caster sugar
1 sheet of ready-rolled puff pastry
1 egg yolk
1 tablespoon milk
400g Christmas Mincemeat (see page 249)
25g flaked almonds
zest of 1 orange
1 teaspoon ground cinnamon
icing sugar, for dusting

Preheat the oven to 200°C/gas mark 6.

Scatter the sugar over the worktop, unroll the pastry and roll it out to 350mm x 225mm.

Whisk the egg yolk with the milk. Spread the mincemeat evenly over the pastry, leaving a 2cm border along the longer edges. Fold one of the longer edges over the mincemeat, then roll the pastry tightly into a sausage shape while gently pressing the pastry into the mincemeat. When you get to the other edge, brush it with milk and egg and press it down to seal in the mincemeat. Press both ends in gently to plump up the roll and chill for at least 30 minutes to firm it. (The mincemeat roll may now be frozen whole or as portioned slices, see below, and kept for up to a month.)

Cut the roll into 12 rounds, each about 3cm thick. Lay them evenly spaced on a large baking tray and flatten them with your hand so they resemble squashed Chelsea buns. Scatter over the flaked almonds and orange zest, sprinkle the ground cinnamon on top and bake for 20-30 minutes until golden brown and the mincemeat sizzles. Leave to cool for 5 minutes; keep them separate so they don't stick together.

Sift icing sugar over the before serving.

CHRISTMAS LIST

Make your Christmas cake
Order your meat
Make a homemade wreath
Buy stocking fillers
Write and send your
Christmas cards
Bake and wrap edible
gifts for your friends
and family
Decorate the tree!

I love the way Christmas both passes on traditons and creates new ones.

SMOKED SALMON TERRINE WITH DILL AND LEMON CREAM

This is the perfect starter for when you have guests coming. You can make it the day before and leave it in the fridge until it is time to serve.

Serves 8

500g cream cheese, softened
80ml double cream
zest of 1 lemon
2 tablespoons lemon juice
3 tablespoons fresh dill, finely chopped
2 tablespoons capers, drained
600g sliced smoked salmon, sliced
sea salt and freshly ground black pepper

To serve

1 bunch watercress, trimmed
brown bread

Make the dill and lemon cream. Place the cream cheese, cream, lemon zest, lemon juice, dill and capers in a food processor, season with salt and pepper and blitz to combine.

Grease an 8cm x 10cm x 20cm loaf tin. Line the base and sides of the tin with cling film, allowing a 5cm overhang on the long sides.

Trim any brown edges from the salmon. Cover the base of the tin with 1 layer of smoked salmon. Using a spatula, spread $^1/_3$ of the cream cheese mixture over the salmon. Add another salmon layer on top, followed by another cream cheese layer. Repeat until the cream cheese mixture is used, finishing with a salmon layer. Fold the cling film over the top, press down gently and refrigerate overnight.

Before serving, turn the terrine out. Remove the cling film, and trim the ends. Serve with watercress and some homemade brown bread.

CELERIAC AND HAZELNUT SOUP

Celeriac and hazelnut are such a great combination. This is a very creamy soup, the hazelnuts add a deep nutty flavour and crunch. Try adding celeriac to creamy mashed potato the next time you cook it.

Serves 6

20g butter
100g onions, chopped
130g potatoes, peeled and chopped
450g celeriac, peeled and chopped
1 litre hot chicken stock
200ml single cream
2 tablespoons chopped hazelnuts
1 tablespoon finely chopped flatleaf parsley
sea salt and freshly ground black pepper

Set a saucepan over a medium and melt the butter. Stir in the onions, potatoes and celeriac, cover and leave to sweat for 10 minutes, checking and stirring every few minutes. Remove the lid and cook for a further 5 minutes, stirring every minute, to help build up the flavour.

Pour the stock over the vegetables and continue to cook until all the vegetable are cooked through.

Add the cream, stir and season to taste with salt and pepper. Blend with a hand blender or food processor until smooth and creamy.

Toast the chopped hazelnuts in a hot oven or in a dry frying pan. Sprinkle a few nuts over each serving of soup together with some parsley.

ORANGE, CINNAMON AND STAR ANISE TURKEY GLAZE

Not only is this glaze perfect for glazing turkey or ham, it also works as a beautiful glaze for non-iced Christmas cakes!

juice of 4 oranges
200g granulated sugar
1 cinnamon stick
1 star anise

Pour the juice of 4 oranges, sugar, cinnamon and star anise into a saucepan set over high heat. Stir every 30 seconds until the sugar has dissolved into the juice.

Bring the liquid to the boil, reduce the heat and leave to simmer for 15 minutes.

Remove the pan from the heat and allow to cool. The syrup will thicken as it cools.

TURKEY TIPS

If you are using a frozen turkey it's best to thaw the bird in the fridge. A turkey will need about 24 hours to thaw for every 1.8-2.25kg. If your turkey is fresh it is best to store it in the fridge if at all possible.

Take the turkey out of the fridge 45 minutes before roasting to allow the meat to relax and come to room temperature, which will make the meat more tender.

To prepare the turkey for cooking remove the giblets from inside the bird's cavity because these cannot be cooked with the turkey. Keep them for when you are making turkey stock or gravy. Wash the cavity and make sure it is completely dry with kitchen paper.

Stuffing that is cooked inside a turkey is definitely tastier than stuffing cooked separately, but you must make sure that the stuffing is cool and fill only half the cavity. Tie the legs together with twine. If you decided to cook the stuffing separately use the juices from the cooked turkey to keep the stuffing moist.

If possible place a wire rack in the roasting tin for the turkey to sit on. This will allow the juices and fat to drain off, and you can use them to baste the turkey while it is cooking to give a tastier meat.

Tuck potatoes around the turkey so they soak up the delicious flavours.

Use a good-quality cranberry or apple jelly as a glaze for the turkey. Use a pastry brush to paint the bird with the jelly and baste every 30 minutes.

Check to see if the turkey is cooked by inserting a skewer into the thickest part of the thigh; the juices should run clear.

When you have taken the turkey out of the oven leave it to rest for 30 minutes with a loose tent of kitchen foil over the bird to keep it warm. This will allow the juices to redistribute themselves, giving tastier meat.

TURKEY COOKING TIMES

You should always allow 15 minutes per 450g, plus an additional 15 minutes.

3.5-5kg	5.5-6.5kg	6.5-8kg	8-9kg	9-11kg
3 hours 20 minutes - 4 hours 40 minutes	4 hours 40 minutes - 5 hours 20 minutes	5 hours 20 minutes - 6 hours 40 minutes	6 hours 40 minutes - 7 hours 20 minutes	7 hours 20 minutes - 8 hours 40 minutes
3 hours - 4 hours 20 minutes	4 hours 20 mins - 5 hours	5 hours - 6 hours 20 minutes	6 hours 20 minutes - 7 hours	7 hours - 8 hours 20 minutes

THE PERFECT ROAST POTATOES

I think Maris Pipers or King Edwards make the best roast
potatoes, as they provide a fluffy inside to your crispy
skin. And yes, goose fat is essential. Go on it's Christmas!

Serves 8

1.8kg potatoes, peeled
3 tablespoons goose fat
3 tablespoons chopped
thyme leaves
sea salt and freshly
ground black pepper

Preheat the oven to 200°C/gas mark 6.

Cut the potatoes in half or in quarters if they are
very big: they should all be similar in size. Put them
into a saucepan of cold salted water, bring to the
boil and cook for 8 minutes. Drain.

Put the goose fat in a roasting tin over a hot hob.
When it is hot, stir in the thyme leaves. Add the
potatoes and season with salt and pepper. Toss in the
fat and cook in the oven for 30 minutes.

MUSTARD GLAZED CARROTS, SHALLOTS AND PARSNIPS

You can add fennel, swede and celeriac to the mix if you
wish. Make the glaze the day before and refrigerate, one
less thing to do on Christmas day!

Serves 6

50g butter
1 tablespoon cider
vinegar
3 tablespoons grainy
mustard
3 tablespoons light brown
sugar
12 shallots, root ends
trimmed
500g carrots, cut into
5cm pieces
500g parsnips, cut into
5cm pieces
sea salt and freshly
ground pepper

Preheat the oven to 200°C/gas mark 6.

Melt the butter and pour it into a bowl. Add the
vinegar, mustard and sugar and whisk together.

Put the vegetables in a roasting tin, pour over the
mustard glaze and mix well. Season with salt and
pepper and cook in the oven for 35-40 minutes or until
tender.

SPICED RED CABBAGE

The colour of this recipe is fantastic, it adds so much flavour to a Christmas table. It will last for up to 4 days in the fridge.

Serves 6

70g butter

800g red cabbage, shredded

$^1/_2$ onion, thinly sliced

1 dessertspoon ground cinnamon

1 teaspoon ground nutmeg

6 cloves

75ml red wine vinegar

70g brown sugar

350g cooking apples, peeled, cored and sliced

sea salt and freshly ground black pepper

Set a large, heavy-bottomed saucepan or casserole dish over a medium heat and add the butter. Add the cabbage and onion, stir well and cook for a few minutes to soften.

Season with salt and pepper and stir in the spices. Add the vinegar and sugar and allow to cook for a further 5 minutes.

Put the apples on top, cover and leave for 10 minutes. Remove the lid, stir and leave to cook for a further 10-15 minutes.

SPICED CRANBERRY SAUCE

You can substitute the fresh cranberries for apricots or plums and this sauce will be equally delicious.

Serves 6

200g granulated sugar
100ml water
400g cranberries
7.5cm piece of fresh ginger
10 whole cloves
1 whole red chilli
1 cinnamon stick

Put the sugar, water and cranberries in a saucepan.

Use the tip of a small teaspoon to peel the fresh ginger, and stud the ginger with the cloves. Add the ginger to the saucepan along with the chilli and the cinnamon stick.

Set the saucepan over a high heat and bring to the boil, stirring every 30 seconds to make sure that the sugar dissolves. When the cranberries have popped, reduce the heat to a simmer and allow to cook for a further 10 minutes.

The cranberry sauce is best served at room temperature. Cranberry sauce will thicken when it is chilled, so if you make it a few days in advance and add a little water to the saucepan before adding the sauce and warm it gently.

VARIATIONS

For spiced orange and cranberry sauce
Replace the with freshly squeezed orange juice.

For spiced plum sauce
Replace the cranberries with quartered and stoned fresh plums.

SAGE, PANCETTA AND DATE STUFFING

This could be looked upon as my Italian influence on my otherwise traditional Irish Christmas lunch. The sweetness from the dates, smokiness from the pancetta and earthiness from the sage make an incredible stuffing.

Serves 8

200g pancetta, chopped

1 large onion, finely diced

3 tablespoons chopped sage

100g dates, finely chopped

600g good-quality pork sausages, skins removed

40g fresh white breadcrumbs

2 tablespoons chopped parsley

1 teaspoon freshly grated nutmeg

sea salt and freshly ground black pepper

Set a frying pan over a medium heat and cook the pancetta for about 4 minutes or until golden. Stir in the onion and cook for a further 5 minutes. Transfer to a bowl.

Stir in the sage, dates, sausagemeat, breadcrumbs, parsley and nutmeg. Season with salt and pepper and mix well.

Makes 24

1 bottle of good red
wine
100g demerara sugar
rind of 1 lemon
rind of 1 orange
stick of cinnamon
3 cloves
splash of brandy

MULLED WINE

Probably the easiest thing for you to make over Christmas — it's brimming with Christmas spices. Add some sloe gin if you have it. Serve with a slice of orange.

Set a large, heavy-bottomed saucepan over a low heat. Add all the ingredients to the pan and stir until all the sugar has dissolved and the wine is hot, but drinkable.

WINTER BERRY SHERRY TRIFLE

I use madeira cake in my trifle as it absorbs all the delicious flavours of the crème cassis and berries and also adds its own flavour. Make sure you buy good quality custard, no tinned custard need enter!

Serves 8

500g frozen mixed berries
70g golden caster sugar
50ml crème de cassis
200g Madeira cake, sliced
250ml mascarpone cheese
1 tablespoon vanilla extract
500ml custard
300ml double cream, softly whipped

Put the berries and sugar in a saucepan over a low heat and simmer for 2 minutes. Stir in the crème de cassis and set aside to cool.

Arrange a layer of Madeira cake slices at the bottom of a large trifle bowl and spoon two-thirds of the berry mix on top.

In a mixing bowl whisk together the mascarpone, vanilla extract and custard until smooth; take care that it does not become too runny. Spoon the custard mixture on top of the cake and berries and top with the whipped cream.

Chill for a couple of hours in a fridge. Just before serving pour the remaining berries on top.

LEMON PASTRY MINCE PIES

You can use the zest of orange if you prefer. Chill your pastry cases in the fridge before you bake, they will be more buttery as a result.

Makes 16-24

melted butter, for greasing
200g plain flour, sifted
zest of 1 lemon
1 tablespoon icing sugar
100g chilled unsalted butter, cubed
1 egg, beaten, plus extra for glazing
Christmas Mincemeat (see page 237)

Preheat the oven to 200°C/gas mark 6. Lightly grease a shallow 24-hole fairy cake tin or a 16-hole muffin tin.

Put the flour, lemon zest, icing sugar and butter in a food-processor and whizz briefly. Add half the beaten egg and continue to blend. You might add a little more egg, but not too much as the mixture should be just moist enough to come together. If you are making the pastry by hand rub the butter into the flour until it resembles coarse breadcrumbs, then, using your hands, add just enough egg to bring it together.

With your hands, flatten out the ball of dough until it is about 2cm thick. Wrap it in clingfilm or put it in a plastic bag and leave it in the fridge for at least 30 minutes or, if you are pushed for time, in the freezer for 10-15 minutes.

On a lightly floured work surface roll out the pastry to 3mm thick. Use a 6cm (or an 8cm cutter if you are using a muffin tin) cutter to cut out 24 circles for the bases, and use a smaller plain or fluted cutter or star cutter to cut out 24 circles or stars for the lids. Re-roll the trimmings if necessary.

Line the holes of the cake tin with the larger pastry rounds. Fill each base with a teaspoon of mincemeat and top with one of the smaller rounds or stars. Brush the tops of the mince pies with beaten egg and cook in the oven for 15-20 minutes.

TURKEY CURRY

I don't know about you but I always cook too much turkey. I was determined to create a curry that would wow me nearly as much as the Christmas dinner. Serve with Basmati Rice, my Raita on page 273 and my Naan Bread on page 272.

Serves 6

3 tablespoons olive oil

1 large onion, finely chopped

4 garlic cloves, finely chopped

5cm piece of fresh ginger, peeled and grated

1 red chilli, deseeded and finely chopped

8 green cardamom pods, pods removed

1 teaspoon ground cumin

1 tablespoon ground turmeric

1 teaspoon garam masala

1 teaspoon ground coriander seeds

2 large potatoes, peeled and diced

1 butternut squash, peeled, deseeded and diced

600ml chicken or turkey stock

125ml yogurt

85ml double cream

1 tablespoon lemon juice

150g turkey, cooked and chopped

1 tablespoon chopped fresh coriander leaves

sea salt and freshly ground black pepper

Set a large casserole over a medium heat and pour in the oil. Stir in the onion, garlic, ginger, chilli, cardamom seeds, cumin, turmeric, garam masala and ground coriander. Cover and sweat for 3-4 minutes until the onions are soft; take care not to burn the spices.

Stir in the potatoes and butternut squash and cook until the potato begins to stick to the bottom of the casserole slightly.

Pour in the stock and bring to the boil. Season to taste with salt and pepper. Reduce the heat and simmer for 10-15 minutes or until the potatoes and butternut squash are tender.

Stir in the yoghurt and cream, then add the lemon juice and turkey. Simmer to heat through, sprinkle with coriander and serve immediately.

CINNAMON AND BERRY GRANOLA BARS

Use any dried berries you wish. If you are not a fan of cinnamon, replace it with 1 teaspoon of vanilla extract.

Makes 12 bars

100g butter, plus extra
for greasing
200g porridge oats
100g sunflower seeds
50g sesame seeds
50g chopped walnuts
3 tablespoons honey
100g light muscovado
sugar
1 teaspoon ground
cinnamon
100g dried cranberries,
cherries or blueberries,
or a mixture

Preheat the oven to 160°C/gas mark 3. Butter and line the base of a 18 × 25cm tin.

Mix the oats, seeds and nuts in a roasting tin and toast them in the oven for 5-10 minutes.

Meanwhile, put the butter, honey and sugar in a saucepan and stir until the butter has melted. Add the oat mixture, cinnamon and dried fruit and mix until the oats are well coated.

Tip the mixture into the tin, press down lightly and bake in the oven for 30 minutes. Leave to cool in the tin, then carefully remove and cut into 12 bars.

WHITE CHOCOLATE, HAZELNUT AND CRANBERRY CHRISTMAS COOKIES

Wrapped in a pretty bag or box these cookies make a lovely edible Christmas gift. You can freeze or refrigerate the dough.

Makes 24 cookies

250g butter, softened
120g caster sugar
300g plain flour
1 teaspoon baking powder
80g white chocolate,
chopped
70g hazelnuts, chopped
70g dried cranberries,
chopped

Preheat the oven to 180°C/gas mark 4.

Put the butter and sugar in a large bowl and cream together with a wooden spoon until pale in colour.

Sift the flour and baking powder into the bowl. Add the chocolate, hazelnuts and cranberries and bring the mixture together to form a dough.

Divide the dough into three pieces and roll each piece into a sausage shape. Chill in the fridge for 1 hour.

Cut each roll into 8 slices and bake in the oven for 10-15 minutes.

INDEX

INDEX

INDEX

INDEX

INDEX

DEDICATION

I dedicate my book to my 3 older siblings (yes I'm the baby!). My brother Jim for always making sure that I walked on the inside of the path and always being their for me through everything. My sister Mairead for being the backbone to our family, your strength is so inspiring and comforting to me, and Niamh for having a true heart of gold. I love you more than words can say and feel so blessed to have such a special closeness with you all. Thank you for all your encouragement and belief.
Family Forever, Clo xxxx

ACKNOWLEDGEMENTS

When creating a cookbook, endless hours of creativity, passion and commitment are given to the project by so many people. Firstly I would like to thank Kyle Cathie, an incredible woman who I look up to immensely. Kyle, you fabulous woman, masses of gratitude for letting me share my recipes, food and above all for believing in me.

Kate Whitaker, photographer, what can I say? A beautiful lady in the truest sense of the meaning. She quietly does her magic while we all stand back in silenced awe. Your wonderful eye has brought my recipes to life. You have such an incredible talent and I hope to be lucky enough to work with you again and again. Lizzie Harris, the kitchen angel, how gorgeous it was to work with you. You are so calm and serene, not to mention a fantastic cook, you need to have your own book — you are too talented not to! Emily Kyd, thank you so much for your great cooking and for making those macaroons in the London summer heat! Penny Markham, prop stylist, thank you for foraging the most beautiful dishes, plates and glasses for my food to fill! Emma Bastow, editor, thank you for your diligence and commitment to the book and for being so patient with me! Lucy Parissi, art direction and design, thank you for the wonderful design. Production team, Gemma John and Nic Jones, thank you!

For all on my home turf, my sister-in-law and best friend Erin McKenna, for your constant encouragement and keep everything afloat in my life! Michael Andrews (aka Arch Angel Michael) for being the most fantastic general manager of the restaurants. All my chefs — Ben, Alberto, Cora, Suzanna, Kamil, Ron, Bischal, Jamille, Ausra, Rachel and Gary, for creating wonderful dishes from my recipes.

Lastly, and above all, I want to thank Peter Gaynor, for being everything...
I love you.